The Power of Money

LOW-RISK INVESTMENT STRATEGIES FOR CANADIANS

The Power of Money

LOW-RISK INVESTMENT STRATEGIES FOR CANADIANS

JERRY WHITE

McGraw-Hill Ryerson

Toronto   Montreal

First published in 1994 by
McGraw-Hill Ryerson Limited
300 Water Street
Whitby, Ontario, Canada
L1N 9B6

Canadian Cataloguing in Publication Data
White, Jerry, 1946-
    The power of money

Text accompanied by disk.
ISBN 0-07-551757-4

1. Investments - Canada.   2. Finance, Personal.
T. Title

EC4521.W55 1994   332.6'0971   C94-932272-5

Publisher: Donald S. Broad
Book and disc packaged by Shaftesbury Books, Toronto
Cover design: Dave Hader, Studio Conceptions
Text design: JAQ
Editorial services provided by Word Guild, Markham, Ontario

Printed and bound in Canada

Contents

LIST OF FIGURES

LIST OF TABLES

Preface

Canada is a large and beautiful country. It has four million square miles, and its 28 million people are perceived by most people from outside Canada as being some of the luckiest on earth. Canadians are largely free, well fed, healthy, safe and educated. We are peacekeepers to the world, generous and giving.

In fact, as I have often said at many of my nearly 200 seminars a year, Canadians have a major advantage over most people in the world. When you as a Canadian awake each morning and look in the mirror, you are probably looking at one of the best people on earth. Whether you were born here or are a Canadian by choice, we are all in this together. Canadians are a great collection of people who deserve the best, because they are the best.

This may sound patriotic and even patronizing to some, but it is how I really feel as a Canadian. Anyone who is not a Canadian, and writes about what Canadians should do with their money, while well-intentioned is still not one of us and doesn't feel what we feel.

They do not know the disappointment, cynicism and anger towards government. They do not feel the oppression of the massive tax assault upon all Canadians. They do not share the concern over the deficits, the misspending on welfare and the lack of economic vision. We know collectively that Canada is one of the best places on earth and should be better. We should have achieved more, built more, invested more and created more.

In 1945, Canada was the fifth-largest military force on earth. Today, in terms of its military strength, Canada really doesn't even belong in the G-7 as Spain and Italy have surpassed us, and Hong Kong is not far behind. We suffer from one of the highest rates of unemployment: 34 per cent of the workforce is illiterate, 44 per cent innumerate and 75 per cent financially incompetent.

The Canada Pension Plan is now in a negative cashflow of at least a billion dollars a year and this number is rising. Canadian savings have fallen, and net disposable income has declined by nearly 10 per cent in five years, yet taxes have risen by 42 per cent since 1986. Between 1982 and 1992, 60 per cent of all taxes collected by Revenue Canada were from those earning $20,000 to $60,000 a year taxable income.

By having effectively destroyed the middle class, the governments have now refocused their aim on those over 65 who control two-thirds of savings and investment and have 50 per cent of the disposable income.

The dollar has declined by nearly 10 per cent in the past 12 months and 19 per cent since 1991. Interest rates — buffeted by $800 billion in federal and provincial debt, the Quebec situation, and a general global lack of confidence in Canada's leadership — have enjoyed a great roller-coaster ride causing havoc with stock markets and mutual funds.

Various governments, by using the lack of the right to property in the Charter of Rights, have enacted legislation to take property away if need be. In June 1993, the federal government passed Bill C-124 — the Exchange Control Act — which contains a clause that lets the government take your assets in a time of national emergency and seize safety deposit box holdings if requested to do so by the International Monetary Fund in the event of a major national fiscal crisis.

In Ontario and British Columbia, the government has passed the Substitute Decisions Act (effective January 1, 1995) that permits the provincial trustee to seize all assets of anyone over 18 who becomes incompetent through accident or sickness, regardless of the wishes of the family. The only protection is to establish an Enduring Power of Attorney over all assets, not just a bank account, to protect yourself. More about this in the chapter on wills and estates. These changes are frightening.

MY VIEW

Let it never be construed that I am anti-Canadian or even excessively critical of Canada. I simply believe we need a context into which financial strategies can be formulated.

Canada was rated Number One on June 1, 1994 by the U.N. survey on the quality of life. Second was Switzerland, third Japan. The U.S.A. was rated eighth.

In contrast to the United States, despite our oppressive taxes, we are still far better off economically.

In *Capitalism without Capital*, Geoffrey Hawthorn points out that in 1990, the richest 1 per cent of families in the U.S. owned 36.2 per cent of the country's private wealth. The next richest 9 per cent owned 36 per cent, and the remaining 89.9 per cent owned one trillion dollars, far less than the richest 1 per cent. The wealth was increasing in the hands of the top 1 per cent and the middle class was in sharp decline. This is a society where immunization and the educational standards of one-third of children are the lowest in the G-7. Thirty million people have no health care.

Canadians have a much better existence. While our health care sucks $90 billion out of the system and is ineffectual and inefficient, it is still universal. If 220 million Americans share one trillion dollars in personal holdings, Canada's 28 million share the same amount with far greater equity. The top 1 per cent of Canadians controls only about 10 per cent of the wealth, and we have savings per capita more than double the U.S. rate, despite sharply lower taxes south of the border.

Canadians are better off and the world recognizes it. Our goal is to protect what we have and to grow it carefully via asset preservation and conservative income growth.

Fear is the dominant factor in our decision-making. We seem less concerned with growth than with preserving our assets and holdings from deflation, taxes and capricious acts of government.

Canadians call me by the hundreds because of their fear of further currency failings and ever-increasing tax onslaught. We know Canadians will inherit one trillion dollars in the next 10 years. No government will let that be transferred untouched and untaxed.

Ontario's "fair" tax commission report suggests both a capital tax on assets while you are alive and an estate tax upon demise. Ottawa thinks this is a smashing idea. They plan a massive two-year overhaul of pension and retirement income legislation insuring a massive tax grab from RRSPs, RIFFs and savings. Ontario increased probate fees 300 per cent to 1.5 per cent of the total estate.

First, we had the clawback of the Old Age Pension, then the elimination of age exemption and capital gains deduction; next there will be changes in the ages you can claim CPP and when you can roll over to RRIFs and contribute to RRSPs.

The budgets show 1993 tax revenues from individuals were $52 billion, $59 billion in 1994, $64 billion for 1995 and $70-plus billion for 1996. *No new taxes, eh???*

Hundreds of thousands of Canadians were confronted with "sticker shock" in 1992 and 1993 as they rolled over GICs and bonds. Canadians lost $6.9 billion in investment income in 1993 alone because they chose to react to the market or do nothing instead of developing a proactive investment plan.

Then they moved this "hot money" from GICs yielding 1 per cent after tax and inflation into mutual funds. The industry grew by 400 per cent in four years. There are nearly 800 Canadian funds and 5,200 U.S. and foreign ones, with 20 to 30 new ones being added each month.

Most did not know what they were buying and why they were buying it. Some chose bond funds because they heard the word "bond" and that meant low risk, they thought. But investment in Canadian bond funds, due to rising interest rates, resulted in losses of up to 10 per cent for the first five months of the year.

The "hot money" began to dump its bank mutual funds in great quantity as GIC rates began to rise. Net losses were $1.5 billion in redemptions in April 1994 alone. This was no-risk/low-risk money and it went back to its home 90 days after mutual funds were purchased.

Canadians need help to succeed in the mid and late 1990s, especially those over age 50 and those with assets and investments in place for their retirement.

Clearly I want you to succeed. I chose to research and evaluate a number of concepts of investing to prove or disprove certain ideas such as asset allocation, diversification and low-risk strategies. The goal was to separate myth from reality. How can we increase our returns, reduce our risk and preserve our capital in this economic, tax and investment environment we call Canada?

This is a new and innovative book with a software disk to allow you to implement what we talk about and be proactive. This is not only a book, but a system for getting things done. This is not empty rhetoric or meaningless clichés. This is hard, cold fact.

Bruce Ramsey of Ram Technologies is a major force in creating the software and making it work to represent my vision of the world.

This book tries to do all of this and cover all the issues of our economic environment — investment strategy, equity selection, mutual fund strategy, international investing, tax planning, insurance, real estate, and estates, wills and trusts — with the goal of conservative and realistic growth and capital preservation.

I would like to thank the tens of thousands of Canadians I speak to each year for the motivation to deal with these issues.

Particularly, I would like to compliment The Financial Forum of Toronto and Vancouver, CFRB radio in Toronto, financial-planning firms, Fortune Financial, The Financial Concepts Group, AIC, J.D. Mason/Cartier Capital, Multi Mutual, T.D. Green Line, Panfinancial Group and Gordon Berger, Equion, Regal Capital, Premier Capital, Kingwest Management and all the staff and partners of J. White & Associates Inc.

Special thanks also to Warwick Publishers and McGraw-Hill Ryerson.

I am noted for my directness, and even rudeness to the Canadian public. If all else fails, we try honesty. This is a book and financial-planning system for those who truly want to succeed in this country. It is a conservative, risk-reduced approach that will greatly assist you in the future. Read this book and use the software. Act now. I wish you well.

Jerry White
October, 1994

Excellence is what we repeatedly do. Therefore, it is not an act but a habit.
Aristotle

ARE YOU A FINANCIAL CONSERVATIVE? SHOULD YOU BE?

The "Conservative" in Conservative Investor has nothing to do with politics or railing against government.

Conservatism is a philosophy of life and a way of investing. It does not mean no risk at all but rather choosing options and strategies that mitigate risk.

Our goal is to first determine if you are a conservative investor. What are your goals and objectives? How do you like to live and make investment decisions? What is your age, education and income? What is your view of life and society? Do you have priorities?

If we can answer these questions, we can be more successful in placing you in the proper category.

We all know that any investments have risk. Even fixed-income securities that are government guaranteed have risk if interest rates fall and taxes rise. The risk is in making no return at all.

About 5 per cent of the population has assets over $500,000. Once they hit 60, their primary investment goal is no longer planning for retirement but asset or capital preservation. They do not wish to lose what they have and believe their capital will be adequate to tide themselves over.

CHAPTER ONE

The Conservative Investor

T he Conservative Investor is usually born with conservative values.

We conducted a nation-wide analysis over the last three years of the behaviour and investment patterns of nearly 2,000 Canadians, in all age and income groups, to learn about their motivation and characteristics so we could answer the question **What is a Conservative Investor?**

We are able to break the consumer market up into many different segments ranging from risktakers at 13 per cent of the population to idealists at 10 per cent. They were asked questions about what money meant to them, how they approach their personal finances and what they worried about and what characteristics they felt contributed most to personal financial success.

The segments broke down as follows:

SEGMENTS AS A PERCENTAGE OF THE ADULT POPULATION

Type of Investor	%	Attitude and Philosophy
Risktakers	13%	Need risk to succeed at anything
The Conservative	19%	Safety, security, responsibility
The Providers	16%	Altruistic, sharing
The Spendthrifts	14%	Live well or die
The Acquisitors	13%	Controlled by money
The Indifferent	14%	Need just enough to get by
Idealists	10%	Not emotionally concerned about money

The largest segment of the population — nearly 20 per cent — is financially conservative. They value security, comfort, being able to help one's children get a college education, and financial security. They worry about making the wrong choices in investments, taking unnecessary risks and being audited by Revenue Canada.

The Conservative Investor is 45-plus with an income above the national average. They believe that friends should not lend to friends, women shouldn't pay on dates, and that you must be financially responsible for yourself.

They tend to have more investment holdings than all other groups, particularly in real estate, bonds, GICs and insurance. Other characteristics and attitudes that dominate the Conservative Investor are:

		Per cent of Responses
1)	It is wrong to desire money too intensely	65%
2)	Tend to be miserly but money wise	60%
3)	Look out for yourself when it comes to money	90%
4)	Always looking for a bargain	60%
5)	Disciplined about spending money	57%
6)	Know how money works, how to use it and how to spend it	68%
7)	Own their own home	91%
8)	Paid off their home	64%
9)	Have no loans and two or less credit cards	60%
10)	Consider themselves traditional and responsible with money	61%

These Canadians are the central theme of the Canadian marketplace. They represent the core values of Canadian society. Thirty per cent hold bonds and blue chip equities. For them, money and their financial competence is their financial security. Over 80 per cent are satisfied with their salary and over 70 per cent believe that it is critical to do financial planning for the future.

Ninety per cent of the financially conservative believe it is better to be safe than sorry. They believe it imperative to hang on to what they have and, as they age beyond 60, they wish to preserve capital as a primary goal.

They seriously dislike the federal government and have little confidence in provincial politicians. The Conservative Investor believes in having a will, doing estate planning and sharing financial information with family.

They want to properly plan for their retirement, pay for their children's education and leave something in their estate for their children.

The Conservative Investor is the core of Canadian society. They are responsible, patriotic and give to charities. They look after their own and take personal responsibility for their future.

Because of this orientation, this group will not necessarily be the richest group of Canadians but they will be the most secure.

SHOULD YOU BE A CONSERVATIVE INVESTOR?

May 1994: Chairman of Marks & Spencer Stores in London — "Canada is a terrible place to do business. The worst country." *The Globe and Mail*, May 25, 1994

May 1994: A major German bank advises clients to steer clear of Canadian investments.

May 1994: A major Dutch bank recommends against Canadian investments.

May 1994: David Li, CEO of the Bank of East Asia: "Canada's economy is in danger of self-destructing. It could crumble under the weight of high taxes, massive public debt and unnecessary government regulations."

April 1994: The Department of Health and Welfare Canada says that, for the first time in its 28-year history, it has had to dip into its accumulated surplus of CPP. The level of early retirements, the agency of population and burgeoning disability claims created a $1.1-billion deficit. The current level of contributory earnings of 5.2 per cent for 1994 will have to rise to 13.5 per cent over the next 10 years or the plan will be broke.

March 1994: Family finances have declined. Average after-tax income per family was $43,359, unchanged from the previous two years and off by 5.1 per cent after inflation and still $2,060 less than in 1989. In fact, since 1974 there has been no increase in net family income after tax and inflation. It is expected to continue to decline for the balance of the decade.

March 1994: Statistics Canada reports Canadians spent $9.9 billion more than they earned last year. How? By saving at lower interest rates and consuming $5 billion in their net savings.

March 1994: Statistics Canada reports that of the total of 143,000 jobs created last year, 10,000 were non-salary jobs in family business, and 86,000 were in self-employed low-income home businesses.

February 1994: The Canadian dollar falls from a 1993 high of 79.33¢ to 72.31¢.

February 1994: The federal budget eliminates the old age exemption at a new threshold for wealth — $49,000. Anything above and the Feds consider you rich if you are over 65. The government eliminates $100,000 capital gains exemption and Ottawa looks to review or eliminate family trusts for tax planning, and produces a White Paper on pension and retirement income. The assault on the over-60 middle class has begun.

3

Perhaps now I have your attention. Either you are a Conservative Investor who wishes to learn more about what to do to stay one and achieve your goals, or perhaps you should become one. This is the only style for financial security for Canadians in the 1990s and the one that will produce the safest long-term investment growth.

THE FACTS
I have assembled a series of charts to adequately summarize our starting point.

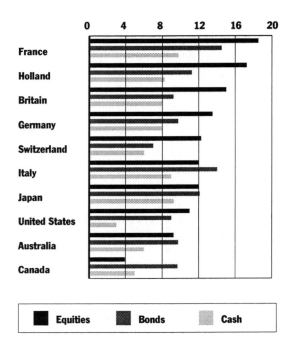

Figure 1.1: Real Return on Investment presents the returns on different investments since 1984. Only in Canada have we created a climate where low-return high-tax GICs and Canada Savings Bonds have outperformed equities.

COMPARING AVERAGE RETURNS BEFORE TAX

	OVER ONE YEAR		OVER FIVE YEARS	
	Rate of return	Present value	Rate of return	Present value
Savings account	0.71%	1,007	4.87%	1,268
5-year fixed term deposit — bank, cashable	6.00%	1,060	9.37%	1,565
5-year GIC — trust company	7.20%	1,072	10.37%	1,638
Canada Savings Bonds	5.39%	1,054	8.70%	1,517
3-month treasury bills	4.97%	1,050	9.31%	1,561
TSE 300 total return index	31.67%	1,317	7.98%	1,468
S&P 500 total return index	8.34%	1,083	18.65%	1,896
Morgan Stanley World total return index—				
World Equity Funds	26.13%	1,261	6.90%	1,396
Consumer price index	1.15%	1,012	3.34%	1,178
Average return for Canadian equity group	18.95%	1,190	12.76%	1,823
Average return for balanced group —				
bonds and equity	19.91%	1,199	10.13%	1,620

Source: Bank of Canada

Table 1.1: Comparing Average Returns before Tax from different products before tax in the past 12 months and over five years. Equities did well domestically and globally before the March sell-off. In the longer term, the returns were from long-term investments in equities and debt. Unlike those in the U.S., Canadians need more liquidity and flexibility and more fixed-income securities. We still need equities and mutual funds, but about 10 per cent less than in the U.S. because of our social/health safety net.

GOLD PRICES PER TROY OUNCE

YEAR	HIGH	LOW
1980	$850	$482
1981	599	391
1982	481	297
1983	509	374
1984	406	308
1985	341	284
1986	438	327
1987	502	389
1988	487	392

5

1989	419	356
1990	425	346
1991	403	341
1992	362	335
1993	407	326
1994	387	*361

* June 1994

Table 1.2: Gold Prices per Troy Ounce 1980 to date shows gold's volatility. It is not for the Conservative Investor — only blue chip gold shares are. Gold is great in teeth, watches and earrings, but not as a portfolio asset.

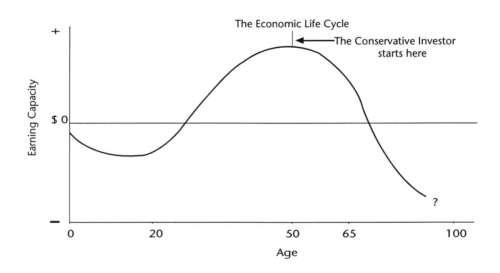

Figure 1.2: Economic Life Cycle and *Figure 1.3:* At Risk — Canadian Household Wealth are perhaps the most important of all. *Figure 1.2* shows your income stream during your life. It peaks at middle age. This is when you must become a Conservative Investor. Your income will not continue at this pace and you must grow and conserve what you have. The famous New Brunswick billionaire, K.C. Irving, established a tax residence in Bermuda and required that at least two of his children do so as well in order to protect himself from what he obviously saw as a massive tax assault on the financially well-off over the next few years.

Figure 1.3 shows us that 71.5 per cent of our assets are in our human capital — our-

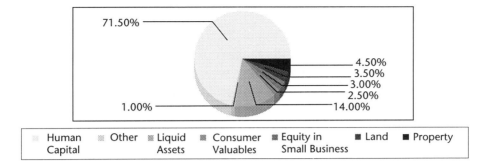

selves as a people. What we have at risk is the 14 per cent of our liquid assets, and to a lesser extent, they are investments in property (houses and investment real estate) and the land under it. This market has flattened out. In Ontario and Quebec, real estate is back to 1984 price levels. In B.C. it is flat and showing little growth. People are now buying accommodation and not investment real estate. Only Victoria, Kelowna, Kingston and London are showing price growth as they attract more Conservative Investor retirees.

Our principal goal is to profit-maximize with low risk the 14 per cent of liquid assets.

RISK

There are many types of risks to worry about.

- Market Timing Risk — Buying mutual funds and bonds and equities at the peak of the market.
- Lost Opportunities — Keeping your money in low-return GICs as other investments rise sharply in value at low tax rates.
- Interest Rate Risk — As rates rise bonds fall, as do equities. As rates fall, equities rise. Most invest the opposite way.
- Speculative Risk — Looking for the big hit, taking unnecessary risk because something may be hot.
- Diversification Risk — You invest vertically in one category such as fixed income only, instead of bonds, cash and equities.
- Lemming Risk — Investing with the mob and lining up to buy whatever is hot. You are buying history, where the market has been, not the future; where it is going.

The Conservative Investor is interested in reducing or eliminating risk. There will always be some risk but we must learn to understand and control it.

7

CONSERVATIVE INVESTOR HINTS

Canadian Dollar Risk

I am regularly asked what to do about protecting yourself against the high-debt structure of Canada and the eventual possibility the country will fall apart if Quebeckers vote for sovereignty. Here is my approach to "bullet-proofing" your currency and using a Conservative Investor strategy:

1) Buy foreign currency denominated mutual funds.

2) Purchase government bonds in U.S. dollars, Swiss francs or Japanese yen.

3) Maximize the foreign content of RRSPs (20 per cent).

4) Buy mutual funds with up to 20 per cent foreign content that still qualify as "Canadian" for your RRSP. This will take your RRSP to 36 per cent foreign, a legal limit.

5) Hold cash in foreign currency in border U.S. banks that are federally insured.

6) Hold up to 10 per cent of your portfolio in collectibles that are liquid in foreign markets. Not baseball cards.

7) For those with $1 million or more, establish an offshore trust in a tax haven.

8) Own foreign real estate in good markets: Hong Kong, Singapore, Orlando, Phoenix, Atlanta, London.

9) Have your relatives, parents or in-laws retire outside of Canada. When they send money to your kids, there is no attribution of the income to you.

10) Keep your skills and résumé current so that if the market crashes and the currency collapses, you will be able to get a transfer to another country. Learn about the Free Trade immigration rules and how they affect your profession. Most people with professional or graduate degrees can go south relatively easily.

CHAPTER TWO

Investment Strategy

Being a native-born Canadian from downtown Toronto, the hotbed of Calvinist Presbyterian financial conservatism, I have grown up with a natural ingrained avoidance of risk. In fact, I was pleased to discover that I met all of the criteria of the Conservative Investor described in the previous chapter.

For the past 25 years as a professor of business at graduate business schools in Toronto, London and New York, I have tried to understand the psychology of the investment market and whether you can actually outperform and outguess the trends in the marketplace. I reviewed all the research literature of the period between 1968 and 1994 to see if the academic view had any practical relevance.

I have tried to summarize the concepts in practical, simple terms so that anyone should be able to follow the concepts. Remember our goal is growth and performance with lower risk with an enhanced element of capital preservation as we get older.

The year 1994 started off well with fine results in Canadian and U.S. equities and equity-based mutual funds. But in January, the big sell-off and profit-taking began in Asia with large drops in Hong Kong, Thailand and the Philippines. Yet the Japanese market began a major comeback contrary to all expectations.

In February of 1994, the U.S. Federal Reserve began to tighten credit with short-term interest rates rising from 3.25 per cent to 4.25 per cent. The yen soared and heavily leveraged investors such as George Soros of the Quantum Fund in New York got massacred. The Canadian bank rate took off and the dollar fell sharply throughout the spring. No one has any sense of what is happening; everyone is losing money and is scared.

IT'S A MAD, MAD, MAD, MAD WORLD

Canadians are now investing in global stocks and bond markets, either directly through $130 billion in mutual funds or through pension plans. Fluctuations in the dollar and interest rates affect their portfolios each day.

Worldwide investing has stretched the boundaries of anxiety. The new phrase is, "I invest, therefore I worry." Currencies are out of control in many governments, and all public events, news and politics affect the performance of the markets and dollar hedges.

In the past, the pros of the stock markets made a fortune, guided by rocket scientists with advanced degrees, largely due to cheap credit and buoyant markets. Since January 1994, these same pros with very sophisticated computer modules have been burned — *badly*.

Those who got "killed" in hedges relied heavily on highly complex computer-driven trading strategies which were used mainly in fixed-income securities. They were designed to enhance yields while "hedging" against interest-rate downturns. These "experts" who managed billions of dollars for just about every Canadian, U.S., Asian and European bank and multinational corporation were so confident of their success that they borrowed heavily to leverage their portion to unheard-of levels of 100-to-1 to develop returns of 40 per cent or more.

They used "arcane" models to trace the interrelationships between seemingly unrelated instruments, linking global markets and economics in ways never dreamed of before. Unfortunately, this elaborate array of markets proved to have unseen flaws when interest rates shot up. The strategies involved too much leverage. They also failed to consider that a serious market spasm could obliterate market liquidity. Computers and new software have produced a closer coordination of world capital markets and allow traders to move money around the world at great speed; this has enhanced market liquidity when things are calm. However, when the markets turned bad, the liquidity disappeared in an instant and the brilliant hedge experts lost it big time.

BEHAVIOURAL FINANCE

Are investors rational decision-makers as suggested in most financial texts? The performance of the markets of late, hedges and the rapid growth of derivatives would suggest that emotion and psychology are important factors as well.

Economists believe that markets are efficient — that is, prices reflect fundamental information available to all, and only change if that information on sales, profits, the economy or competition changes, not in response to the whims and emotions of investors.

Behavioural finance suggests why people are likely to be trend followers. Some give too much emphasis to recent data and not enough to long-run averages or statistical odds. Investors also like to be fashionable, buying what's in this year.

Last year, it was Asia and emerging markets. As a result, the investors feel they have made prudent choices because they believe they have done what other sensible people have done even if they lose money.

Behavioural finance uses two measures of whether the market and consumers are overly optimistic or pessimistic. These are the discounts or premiums on closed-end mutual funds and the volume of initial public offerings (IPOs).

The more people will pay for closed-end funds, the more optimistic they are, the more the market may be overvalued. If investors overpay for IPOs, then they are over-optimistic as well.

Prospect theory is another element of behavioural finance. It shows that people weigh prospective losses greater than actual losses and will hold onto money-losing investments longer than is prudent. Apparently people will pay heavily to avoid loss. That is why they buy mutual funds. Yet the best way to reduce your downside is to buy the market index rather than many funds themselves, something that few people do.

TIME FOR A SIGH OF RELIEF

The 1994 stock market's slide was just a typical correction. The drop was 9.7%, versus an average decline of 9.5%

Stock market declines for the past 50 years

5% or more	127
10% or more	33
15% or more	16
20% or more	9

RAISING YOUR RETURN WITHOUT RAISING YOUR RISK

The answers on the surface are relatively simple. If we diversify our portfolio, cut our debt and costs, trim our taxes, do proper investment and financial planning, then good things can happen.

Risk Return and Volatility

Table 2.1 shows that venture capital has the same speculative risk as gold, but four times the return since 1945.

The higher the risk index, the greater the threat of loss. The key number is the inflation-adjusted return.

Table 2.1

	ANNUAL RATES OF RETURN 1945-1992		
		INFLATION-ADJUSTED RETURN	
	Return	Return	Risk
Emerging-market	16.0%	11.5%	29.6
Venture capital	15.9	11.4	35.4
Japanese stocks	15.9	11.4	29.2
Small-cap stocks	13.5	9.0	25.7
Europe/Asia stock	12.7	8.2	26.5
S&P 500 index	11.7	7.2	16.5
Art	8.5	4.0	15.0
Real estate	7.3	2.8	4.0
Corporate bonds	5.4	0.9	6.2
Long-term bonds	4.9	0.4	9.7
Gold	4.9	0.4	26.0
Treasury bills	4.8	0.3	3.2
Silver	4.2	–0.3	56.2
Inflation	4.5	—	—

CLASSIC INVESTMENT ERRORS TO LEARN FROM

I have produced below a list of classical mistakes made by Canadian investors with the theme that if we make fewer errors we are less likely to increase our risk or lose capital. These are based on observation, reader and listener comments, our own empirical research, and suggestions from brokers and financial planners with whom I work. This will lead into several concepts that we know work — asset allocation and diversification.

The White Sin List

1) Trading in or out of the "hotly" traded shares: Based on the view that valuable information about the most closely followed stocks somehow escapes the attention of the stock market and still has the power to affect the stock market price. It doesn't and this is a fool's game.

2) Buying history — last year's winners: If a stock hits a new high or has a major announcement, people mistake this for a trend. It probably means the trend is over by the time you find out about it.

3) Getting in because everybody is: This usually means it's the time to get out.

4) Selling because the stock or mutual fund will never come back: If it's gone down 15 per cent and it's blue chip, keep it. If it's technology, let it go down 25 per cent and it can come back. If a mutual drops 20 per cent, it's time to sell. The best strategy is to pick and stick for at least 70 per cent of your portfolio.

5) Being confused by analysts: In a bull market the research of analysts can offer valuable insights, but in a down market, if they identify a stock or fund as a hold, it's a sell.

6) Buying initial public offerings: They are roller-coasters. If you want to buy it, wait at least a year.

7) Avoiding the trendy traps:
   a) Faddish restaurant companies
   b) New Real Estate Investment Trusts (see Real Estate)
   c) Initial Public Offerings of new software companies
   d) Emerging markets — Vietnam, Shanghai, Poland, Turkey

8) Tally up your big bills for the next few years: That amount of cash should not be in high-risk investments but in liquid ones for easy access. This includes college, medical, braces.

9) No floor or ceiling in equities: For some who are 50 years of age, the ceiling for equities is 50 per cent of the portfolio and the floor is 25 per cent.

10) Failing to read the prospectus on the fund: Stay away from words like "opportunity" and "frontier" — these mean great risk.

11) Overemphasizing the tax consequences of investments: Investing is quality of return and is risk-return driven — not tax-consideration driven.

12) Not having a will because you think you are immortal: We all need a will and an enduring power of attorney and an estate plan if you have any assets (see chapter on wills).

13) Denying retirement realities: A 1992 survey in Toronto by benefit experts Towers Perrin found that 75 per cent of us expect the same standard of living on retirement, but only 25 per cent of Canadians have a retirement plan and 40 per cent of us are saving less than $1,000 a year towards retirement. This situation is especially severe for women.

14) Fearing the wrong risks: Which is a greater risk — 3.5 per cent return on a GIC before tax and inflation, or 27 per cent capital gain on a blue chip equity? Fear of trading is a greater risk than not trading and incurring dormant money losses all the time.

15) Misreading the market fundamentals: Undervalued, value stocks that are cheap when you look at dividend yield earnings and basic fundamentals are better investments than most. The famous University of Chicago business school study of value investing found in 1992 that value stocks consistently

outperform growth stocks over time and hold up better in a market correction. We look for companies whose current price/earnings multiples are 25 per cent below similar companies in their industry.

16) Trusting the Touts: White's law is that "everything is less than it seems." When someone is touting a front-running stock or mutual fund, it should fall in the near future. This includes most business and financial press. If expectations are too high, they are usually unrealistic.

17) Making a mistake globally: International mutual funds invest globally outside of Canada. Global funds have foreign and Canadian stocks and bonds. Therefore, when you invest internationally, exclude the funds that have Canadian content in your foreign diversification.

18) Reaching for the stars: Some people increase their risk by reaching for every front runner and new investment that comes out. It doesn't work. Stay away from the hyped stocks, as well. I know in watching *Wall Street Week* on PBS these past 10 years that research shows the average recommended stock had actually lost 1.6 per cent relative to the market.

19) Never give up totally: You don't lose money on an investment until you sell. If by chance the mutual fund goes down remember you buy equity, international and balanced funds as a long-term hold and not as a speculative equity.

20) International diversification is not a guaranteed protection against loss; with global trading and real-time computer technology, the markets are moving in closer and closer unison. In 1990, Asia markets had only 30 per cent to 50 per cent correlation with North American performance. Today, it is closer to 70 per cent and likely to rise. Emerging markets are less liquid than North American and more closely held by large corporations and banks. Only European markets show signs of independence and are breaking away.

21) In a major market sell-off, don't expect miracles from anyone: Value stocks will do better in a recovery, but they will fall in a sell-off — 50 per cent of this year's losses were from overseas investing. Bonds are moving closer in sync with stocks.

22) Putting your eggs in a market timing or so-called asset allocation fund because of their ability to move funds quickly: In reality, in the spring 1994 market sell-off, their performance was less than advertised. "Market-timing funds," as they are called, have not reduced risk or enhanced returns.

23) Investing in over-hyped sectors such as high tech, gambling or biotechnology: These markets get saturated quickly and don't go on forever.

24) Buying into any investment category because they look cheap now compared to last year: It probably means they are finished as a group.

25) Rushing back to Japan because it is up: The stocks are selling at a multiple of 60 times earnings and still do not reflect all the Japanese bad news, especially the political news.

26) Using dollar-cost averaging to make up for past mistakes: Research shows that dollar-cost averaging works over the long term, but only if the stock only fluctuates as much as the market in general. If it does work, dollar-cost averaging is not that useful. In fact, research from the Wright State College at Dayton, Ohio shows that lump-sum investing — putting the money into the market quicker — is superior over time.

No Place To Hide?
World markets seem to be most in step with each other when volatility is greatest. Correlation among markets is measured here on a scale of 0 to 1, where 1 indicates markets track each other perfectly and 0 means they are completely independent. Volatility is measured on the basis of "standard deviation"—how much prices vary from the mean.

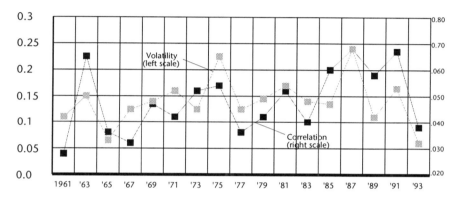

Figure 2.1: No Place to Hide?

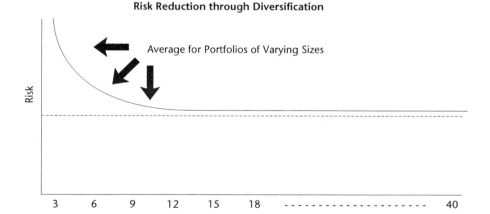

Figure 2.2: Risk Reduction through Diversification. The greater the diversification in a portfolio, the lower the risk and the fewer the swings in returns.

15

STRATEGIES TO REDUCE RISK

1) Investment Strategies

Are you sitting on the sidelines waiting for the market correction or the end of the slump? The potential losses from continuously waiting for the smoke to clear can at times produce even greater losses.

As long as your investment plan is long term — say, five to 10 years — you should be investing even in periods of market uncertainty. Here are the four best-known variations:

a) Dollar-Cost Averaging

In this basic form of periodic investing, you put a set amount each month — say $200 — into a mutual fund or stock portfolio. I already mentioned earlier that lump-sum investing works better. With dollar cost, we buy more as prices fall investing the continuous $200. Therefore, we obtain more shares or, if prices rise, we still invest $200 and obtain fewer shares. This keeps your average share price relatively low.

b) Progressive Dollar-Cost Averaging

A more advanced version of the above process: We avoid the chief drawback of investing the same amount all the time — inflation. With progressive dollar cost, we increase our contribution, say, every six months, by a fixed percentage — perhaps 10 per cent. This will beat inflation, which should average 3 per cent for the next five years.

c) Value Averaging

This system requires you to invest whatever you need to achieve your investment goal.

Let's say you need $9,000 in three years for a downpayment on a house. You first open a fund account with, perhaps, $200. Next, with the help of a financial calculator or compound interest tables found in your local library's reference section, you determine that your account's value must increase $200 a month to reach your target. The actual amount you invest each month will change as stock prices fluctuate. For example, if the market is flat during the month you open your fund account, you simply invest an additional $200 in the second month, bringing your account's value to $400. On the other hand, if your fund's value falls by 12.5 per cent during the second month, your account will dip to $350. Your third investment must then be $250, since your game plan calls for your account to be worth $600 in month three. However, if stocks rise in the second month, boosting your balance to $470, your third contribution need be only $130.

What if the value of your holdings rises so rapidly that your account's value exceeds your monthly target? In that case, value averaging calls for you to sell some shares. Thus, if your account increased to $700 in the third month, you would dump $100 of your holdings. Of course, your profit would be taxable. Therefore, you might prefer a modified value-averaging strategy called *no-sell value averaging*. With this technique, when your portfolio value exceeds the target, you simply do nothing that month.

Value averaging beats dollar-cost averaging roughly 90 per cent of the time, says Michael Edleson, a professor at the Harvard Business School and the author of *Value Averaging: The Safe and Easy Strategy for Higher Investment Returns*. For example, in order to accumulate $49,408 as shown in the table below, you would have had to invest $24,000 from 1984 to '93 if you used dollar-cost averaging, but $23,540 with value averaging. Admittedly, that $450 saving would have been slim. Still, your money would have worked more efficiently, delivering both higher returns and a lower average cost per share.

Table 2.2

IF WE INVESTED IN THE AVERAGE PERFORMANCE OF CANADIAN EQUITY FUNDS FROM 1984-1993

STRATEGY	Monthly Contribution	Total Amount Invested	Portfolio Value	Average Annual Return	Average Cost per Share
Value averaging	Varies	$23,540	$49,408	15.10%	$20.88
Dollar-cost averaging	$200	24,000	49,408	13.83%	21.29
Constant-ratio plan	200	24,000	40,407	9.89%	27.98
Variable instalment	200	24,000	40,297	9.85%	29.29

Value averaging does have one serious drawback. Because you must adjust monthly contributions, you may get caught having to make huge investments when you don't have the money.

d) Constant-Ratio Planning and Variable Instalments

These two extremely conservative methods call for you to balance an equity fund against a less aggressive one, such as a money-market fund.

With constant-ratio planning, you first decide how much risk you can take, then allocate your monthly investment between the two funds accordingly. Let's say you decide to split a $200 monthly investment evenly between a stock fund and a money fund. If equity prices rise, you eventually will have to shift money from your stock fund to your money fund to reestablish your 50:50 ratio. Investment experts recommend that you rebalance your portfolio whenever the ratio gets five percentage points out of whack — in our example, whenever the value of either fund rises to 55 per cent of your portfolio.

Obviously, when stocks are rising, as they were from 1984 to 1993, the more risk you're willing to take when you set the ratio, the more money you will make.

With the variable-instalment strategy, you start out by dividing your monthly investment equally between the funds. Then, when one fund lags behind the other, you direct your entire contribution to it. That way, you buy more shares when they are cheap and avoid putting money into investment categories that may be temporarily overvalued.

Let's again assume you decide to invest $200 a month in a stock and a money fund. You start out by putting $100 into each. Whenever the stock fund's share price drops by an amount that you have determined in advance — say, 5 per cent — you put all of your next monthly investment into that fund. Conversely, if its share price rises 5 per cent, you invest all your next monthly instalment in the money fund. From 1984 to 1993, if you had invested a total of $24,000 using this 5 per cent variable-instalment method, your portfolio would have grown to $40,297. Like the constant-ratio method, variable-instalment would have earned you about $9,000 less than straight dollar-cost averaging, but would have carried less risk.

Since no one expects the next decade to be a replay of the 1984-93 bull market, using a periodic investment plan to add money to your mutual funds may be wise. Because these strategies force you to buy when share prices are low, they get their best results in choppy markets that have prolonged upward trends.

2) Playing the Indexes

Mutual fund managers have tried to outperform the markets over time. Yet in the past decade, fewer than 5 per cent have. Therefore, if we can't beat the market, we join by purchasing the aggregate measures of market performance called indexes which we have listed in the table below.

Traditionally, index funds were used by institutional investors who wanted to diversify without doing worse than the market. Currently, there are nearly 90 different indexes available worldwide.

The appeal of the index fund isn't obvious as they plod along doing no better or worse than the market. But in the long term, they produce steady wins. The only research on performance available, which is from the U.S., shows that, since 1988, only five of 1,543 funds surveyed beat the market index. In fact, in a New York University study of fund performance from 1965 to 1989 showed that a diversified portfolio of large company, small company and bond index funds yielded returns 1.4 per cent higher than managed funds per annum but with obviously less risk, no capital threat and little care or management.

18

AN INDEX OF THE INDEXES

Dow Jones Industrial Average The oldest and most well-known benchmark, the Dow represents only 30 companies. It reflects the market moves in a given day, but only represents 20% of the market, which is comprised of some 6,500 companies. Since Dow companies are weighted by stock price instead of capitalization, it can assign equal value to companies of vastly different sizes.

STANDARD & POOR'S 500 The S&P represents 500 companies — almost all large-capitalization stocks traded on the New York Stock Exchange — but these make up 80% of the market's overall value. A committee periodically adds or subtracts companies from the list based on which ones are dominant in various industry sectors. The S&P 400, despite its billing as a mid-cap index, also tends to be skewed toward bigger companies.

RUSSELL 3000 Russell divides up the market into 3,000 stocks representing 98% of the total equity market capitalization. The top 1,000 form a large-cap index (Russell 1000), and the bottom 2,000 form the widely used Russell 2000 for small-cap stocks. Because the Russell indexes are calculated purely by size — not by committee — some argue they are truer reflections of given segments.

NASDAQ COMPOSITE It lists all the companies in the National Market System — stocks that are traded only over-the-counter and not on an exchange. These tend to be small companies, which graduate to the NYSE or AMEX as they grow. Notable exceptions such as Microsoft and MCI distort this benchmark, making it more mid-cap index than small-cap.

WILSHIRE 5000 This index truly does represent all 6,500 stocks traded in the U.S. for which price data are available (there were only 5,000 when it started). Wilshire breaks these down into large-cap (Wilshire 750), mid-cap (Wilshire Next 1750), and small-cap indexes.

TSE 300 This index measures the top 300 stocks in Canada. It is particularly biased towards resources (18%), but is a better measure of market trends than the more limited TSE 35 which is designed to parallel the Dow Jones.

We can buy indexes and index bonds that produce pleasant low-risk returns of 10 per cent to 14 per cent per annum. Since fewer than 5 per cent of equity mutual funds have outperformed the Standard & Poor's 500, this is the lowest risk route to follow.

3) Asset Allocation the Easy Way

Please fill in the following to get your proper portfolio asset allocation.

STEP 1: STOCKS			STEP 2: BONDS		
AGE	POINTS	SCORE	AGE	POINTS	SCORE
Under 40	10	————	Under 40	10	————
40–60	5	————	40–60	5	————
60-plus	0	————	60-plus	0	————
NET WORTH		————	NET WORTH		————
Under $200K	7	————	Under $200K	7	————
$200K–$1 million	5	————	$200K–$1 million	5	————
$1-3 million	3	————	$1-3 million	3	————
INCOME		————	INCOME		————
Under $100K	5	————	Under $100K	5	————
$100K–$1 million	7	————	$100K–$1 million	7	————
$1-3 million	10	————	$1-3 million	10	————
RISK TOLERANCE		————	RISK TOLERANCE		————
Low	0	————	Low	0	————
Medium	5	————	Medium	5	————
High	10	————	High	10	————
OPTIMISM		————	OPTIMISM		————
Low	0	————	Low	0	————
Medium	5	————	Medium	5	————
High	10	————	High	10	————
TOTAL		————	TOTAL		————
(Enter on line 1 of Step 3)		————	*(Enter on line 3 of Step 3)*		————
100 minus (Total x 2)			100 minus (Total x 2)		

STEP 3: INVESTMENT MIX

Line 1:	————	%	
Line 2:	————		
Line 3	————		
Line 4: (Line 3 x line 2)	————	%	Bonds
Line 5:	————		
Line 6: (Line 5 x line 2)	————	%	Cash

YOUR INVESTMENT MIX

$———— (x line 1)	$————	Stocks
$———— (x line 4	$————	Bonds
$———— (x line 6)	$————	Cash

Age: Since young people can afford to take more risk, score 10 points if you're 40 or under, 0 points if you're 60 or over.

Net Worth: The more you have, the less risk you need to take. Score 7 points if you have under $200,000, and 5 if you're between $200,000 and $1 million.

Income: This is the inverse of net worth. The more income you have, the more risk you can afford. Score 5 points for under $100,000 and 10 for over $1 million.

Risk Tolerance: This one's up to you. Can you afford to let your investments sit for at least five years? Can you be productive at work when your stocks are down? Score 10 for a high risk tolerance, 0 for an extremely low one.

Optimism: This is how you feel about the economy and the stock market for the coming year, not your own personal optimism. The more optimistic you are, the more you should be in stocks.

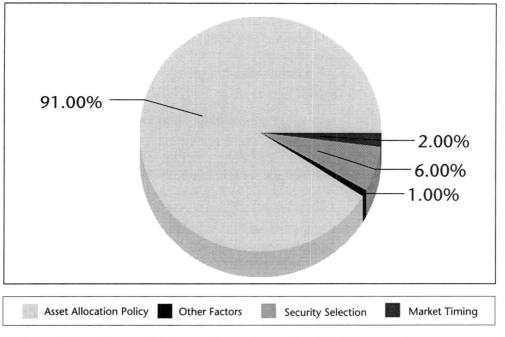

Source: Brinson, Singer, and Beebower. "Determinants of Portfolio Performance,"
Financial Analysts Journal, May–June 1991.

Figure 2.3: Determinants of Portfolio Performance

PORTFOLIO1926–1992 AVERAGE	
100% Stock/0% Bond	10.4%
90% Stock/10% Bond	10.0%
70% Stock/30% Bond	9.2%
50% Stock/50% Bond	8.1%
30% Stock/70% Bond	6.9%
10% Stock/90% Bond	5.5%
0% Stock/100% Bond	4.8%

Table 2.3: Asset Allocation Performance Using Market Averages 1926-1992

Asset allocation truly works. All major studies in the field, including the results shown above, indicate that between 85 per cent and 91 per cent of performance is determined by how we develop the mix appropriate for our needs. The specific products we select account for only 6 per cent to 10 per cent of the result. This preoccupation with specifics is a relatively meaningless act in the total picture.

The table on asset allocation lets you customize weighting for long-term decisions. There is no optional weighting except the one that is appropriate for your specific needs. Our goal is to reduce risk and enhance returns. Therefore, risk is person specific and not general.

There are, however, some general rules of thumb that do work.

At the top end the most equity content anyone should have is 75 per cent, regardless of age, and the lowest level is 25 per cent. We simply have to customize the content weighting to ourselves between 25 per cent and 75 per cent. My experience shows that the majority of so-called conservative investors are, in fact, not true conservatives; they are simply not knowledgeable and make decisions based on their past experience. They will traditionally carry between 0 per cent and 10 per cent in equities, have poor returns, and never meet their targets. This is not low risk or conservative. It is simply wrong.

4) Diversification — The Investment Risk Hierarchy

High Range
Commodities
Futures
Options
High-risk Bonds (Junk)
Gold and Precious Metals
Sector Mutual Funds

High Middle Range
Investment Quality Corporate Bonds
Blue Chip Stocks
Speculative Small Company Growth Stocks
Real Estate Limited Partnerships

Mid Range
Precious Metal Mutual Funds
International Equity and Bond Mutual Funds
Domestic Growth Equity Mutual Funds
Balanced Mutual Funds
Bond Funds

High Low Range
Government of Canada Bonds
Money Market Mutual Funds

Low Range
T-Bills
Bank Deposits — Insured

TYPES OF DIVERSIFICATION AND WHY

In my long-term analysis of Canadian investment behaviours, we looked at our sample going back to 1980 of the 10-year performance of Canadian investments. We found that most investors obtain low yields partially due to improper asset allocation and partially because of the lack of diversification.

We know that diversification spreads risk. The average performance of our 10-year investors was heavily affected by the tendency to invest vertically; that is, in one category of investments — fixed-income securities. Yet when we invested horizontally with proper diversification in each category of our portfolio, we found that over a 10-year period the net growth was 46 per cent greater than for those who invested in an undiversified way. This occurred despite the fact that fixed-income securities were still top performers before tax and inflation during the period measured 1980 to 1990.

Types

a) Company Diversification

Buying many different equities. Our chart shows that at 15 stocks, we have eliminated most of the systematic risk of the market.

b) Industry Diversification

All industries have cycles when they are in and out of favour because of changing economic and business conditions. Therefore, we need to diversify by industry to mitigate risk.

c) Geographic Diversification

This does not just mean investing across Canada or the U.S.A. — it means globally. Although I said earlier markets are being more closely aligned, the alignment is not perfect and we can reduce risk by investing in markets that are more independent and less affected by North American trends.

d) Diversified Companies

When we meet blue chip stocks or high-end equity mutual funds, we should read the prospectus, or Bell Charts, the most complete Canadian mutual fund source table, to determine the size and status of companies in the fund. The larger and more diversified the companies, the lower the probability of a major downturn or collapse.

e) Cluster Investing

A little-known concept developed in 1991 which indicates that although you might purchase eight to 15 stocks or eight different mutual funds, you might still be too heavily located in one or two investment clusters such as growth stocks or government bonds. The concept presents five low-risk clusters: basic industries, growth, oil and utilities and consumer/cyclical. A portfolio from each of the five should aid in reducing risk and stabilizing the portfolio over time.

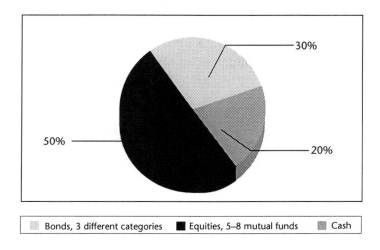

Figure 2.4: Conservative, Low-Risk Portfolio with Proper Diversification, 40 and Under

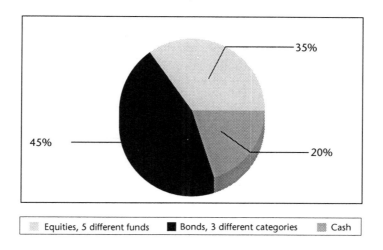

Figure 2.5: Conservative, Low-Risk Portfolio Ages 40 to 60, Proper Diversification and Asset Allocation

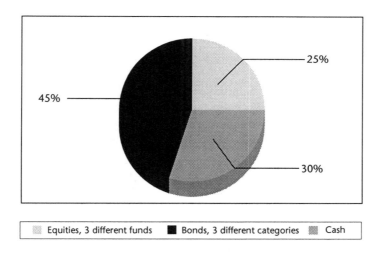

Figure 2.6: Conservative, Low-Risk Portfolio Age 60-Plus, Proper Diversification and Asset Allocation

CURRENCY RISK

Investors are always asking me about the risk of the Canadian dollar. Table 2.4 shows the risk we have in our currency had we invested offshore in foreign currencies. This is only worthwhile for high-net-worth individuals and for those who can meet the minimum threshold levels for setting up foreign accounts.

Table 2.4

FOREIGN CURRENCIES AND GOLD VS. THE CANADIAN DOLLAR: DECEMBER 1970 – MAY 1994			
	CUMULATIVE RETURNS VS. C$	CURRENT INFLATION	10-YEAR BOND*
Swiss Franc	+300.0%	+3.6%	4.22%
Japanese Yen	+345.5%	+1.9%	3.43%
German D-Mark	+195.3%	+3.9%	5.66%
Dutch Guilder	+162.2%	+2.0%	5.77%
Austrian Schilling	+193.9%	+4.1%	5.90%
British Sterling	−20.3%	+1.7%	6.92%
U.S. Dollar	+37.3%	+3.0%	5.56%
Gold	+1,250%	—	—

*10-year government bond yields. In local currency.

Source: J.P. Morgan, *The Economist*

Earlier, I recommended foreign-denominated Canadian bonds, offshore bank accounts and bond funds with Canadian currency hedges built into them. Clearly, Canadians have suffered badly over the past 24 years with respect to the Japanese, German and Swiss. We are even in a declining situation with the U.S. Since we don't want to lose purchasing power, to preserve our capital we need global diversification, particularly in one or two foreign markets listed above. I like having U.S. accounts, or ones in Caribbean, for travel and for offshore trusts.

The Channel Islands, Cayman, Turks and Caicos Islands, Switzerland, Bermuda, Cyprus and Malta are just a few of the better-known offshore locations. Accounts here are managed by major banking groups such as Barclays, Rothschild, Union Bank of Switzerland, Morgan Stanley and Credit Suisse. You'll need a minimum of U.S.$10,000 to $100,000 to start, depending on the bank and country. They often have bond funds in Swiss currency and management fees are low at 0.9 per cent to 2 per cent of the total investment annually.

This is a long-term investment of five to 10 years, ideal for those over 50 and part of an estate plan or offshore trust, if possible. This will cost $7,000 to $15,000 to set up and is valuable for those with $1 million or more to shelter. But you don't have to be rich to take part. But take part you must, and be aggressive about this.

DEBT RISK

We are all aware that debt offers substantial risk. I believe in low leveraging for the financially secure — that is, if you have a strong cash flow, secure job, no debt and the need to produce superior returns. Borrowing to invest is a reasonable approach as debt interest is fully deductible and you should keep it under 20 per cent of your net worth. You should be able to borrow at prime for this purchase, so your cost of money will be half-prime. Both the Bank of Montreal and National Trust have been very aggressive about investor lending.

Using credit card debt is, of course, not a low-risk strategy for the Conservative Investor. The cost of money is exceptionally high. For a bank credit card at 15 per cent, you would need to grow yield on investments of 25 per cent if you are at the 40 per cent marginal tax rate. Department store cards with 33 per cent rates are far worse. Obviously, we need to reduce credit-card debt as a primary risk reduction strategy. I prefer the new debit cards as they are just like writing a cheque. You spend what you have and nothing more.

DEBT AND LEVERAGE RISK

Shakespeare wrote in *Hamlet* 400 years ago, "Neither a borrower or lender be".

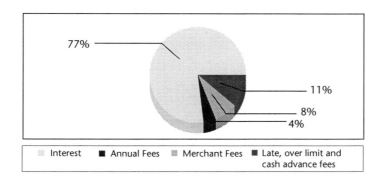

Figure 2.7: Charge It — Where Money Is Made on Credit Cards

The dangers of taking on debt should be obvious to any Conservative Investor. Debt at times is unavoidable for cars, homes, education and investing. The issue is the difference between consumption debt and investment debt, what is deductible for income taxes and how much is appropriate for your overall financial plan.

Credit Card Debt — Consumption Debt: Expensive, nondeductible interest expense, a major cause of financial overcommitments and impulse buying.

Car Loans: Necessary for most to buy cars, important if the car is for business purposes as it may be partially deductible. Avoid long-term loans (over three years). So-called 2.9 per cent financing is usually on the nondeclining balance equivalent to 11.5 per cent interest.

Home Equity Lines of Credit: The lowest cost of borrowing for investors with interest being deductible for tax purposes. Many lenders will accept the mutual funds as collateral on the loan and will not need the house as collateral, a lower-risk approach.

Investment Debt or Margin: Rates are usually at prime — reduces the return on investments but adds to the total amount invested and therefore increasing total after-tax cash flow.

DEBT BY AGE

20 to 40 Years of Age

- Stick to one or two credit cards
- Pay all bills promptly to build credit worthiness
- Put at least 25 per cent down when buying a home
- Use First-Time Home Buyer's Plan via RRSP
- Purchase Labour-Sponsored Venture Capital Corp. using bank loan for RRSP
- Document all family loans and costs
- Consider a variable-rate mortgage to conserve cash

40 to 50 Years of Age

- Pay off credit cards each month
- Buy cars for cash or lease
- Consider a five- or seven-year mortgage if rates stabilize
- Establish a home equity line of credit for emergency
- Leverage to 20 per cent of net worth to build retirement holdings

Age 60-Plus

- Determine your long-term cash flow needs
- Pay off all loans
- Avoid margin
- Use home equity if borrowing needed
- Consider systematic withdrawal plans from mutual funds or from home equity — not reverse mortgages

HEDGES, FUTURES, SWAPS AND OPTIONS

I do not wish to spend a great deal of time discussing the benefits of these concepts. I believe they have value for very sophisticated investors and those very serious about risk reduction. But since hedging and derivatives are increasing in usage and importance, it is important to know what they are and how they work.

Definitions of Financial Terms Related to Risk

Arbitrage: A form of hedged investment meant to capture slight differences in the prices between two securities that should be related. The classic example of arbitrage would be buying gold in London and selling it at a higher price in New York. Many hedge funds specialize in various forms of arbitrage; for example, in the relationship between the common stock and the preferred stock of the same company. Usually the price discrepancies are small, but the investment returns are amplified using leverage.

Derivatives: A broad class of transactions whose value is based on, or derived from, a financial market like stocks, interest rates or currencies. Hedge funds have become big users of derivatives to take large positions, either as outright investments or as hedges, quickly and secretly. Derivatives can also be a way of investing with leverage because many derivative transactions require little or no up-front cash payments.

Hedge Fund: A flexible investment fund for rich people and institutions. The minimum investment is typically $1 million and the manager usually receives 20 per cent of the profits. Hedge funds can use virtually any investment technique including short-selling — that is, borrowing shares and selling them in hopes of benefiting from a decline in prices — and heavy borrowing, or leverage, neither of which is allowed for mutual funds.

Hedging: A strategy for protecting against financial risk by taking two positions that offset each other if prices change. Hedge funds originally tried to protect themselves by purchasing some stocks long and selling others short. If the stock market falls, the short positions would be worth more, but the long positions would lose money. If the market gains, the reverse would be true. The fund would make money, not because of the overall market movement, but because the stocks it bought long would do better relative to the ones it sold short. Today, not all hedge funds hedge.

Leverage: A way to amplify the potential gain or loss of an investment, usually by investing with borrowed money. For example, a fund with $100 of its own cash might borrow $900 — making it "highly leveraged," allowing it to buy $1,000 in bonds. If the bonds rise by 10 per cent, or $100, the fund would effectively earn a 100 per cent return on its initial investment, far greater than the $10 it could have earned if it had used only its own cash to buy just $100 in bonds. Of course, if bond prices fall by 10 per cent, the fund's entire investment would be wiped out after paying back its $900 loan.

Margin Calls: A demand for more collateral by a brokerage firm that has lent money to an investor. Investors are said to be taking a margin loan when they borrow money, but put up stocks or bonds as collateral. But when the value of those securities falls, the lender calls for more collateral to cover it if the borrower defaults. If the margin call is not met, the broker may sell the collateral he does hold to pay off the loans.

Short-Selling: A way to bet that the price of a stock, or other security, will go down. A hedge fund would borrow the stock from a brokerage firm and sell it in the market, hoping to buy it back for a lower price and return it to its owner. Stocks bought the normal way are said to be owned "long."

A Derivatives Glossary

Call: An option giving the holder the right, but not the obligation, to buy a specific quantity of an asset for a fixed price during a specific period.

Cap: A contract that protects the holder from a rise in interest rates or some other *underlying* (see below) beyond a certain point.

Delta: The rate at which the price of an option changes in response to a move in the price of the underlying. If an option's delta is 0.5 (out of a maximum of 1), a $2 move in the price of the underlying will produce a $1 move in the option.

Floor: A contract that protects the holder against a decline in prices below a certain point.

Forward Contracts: A contract obliging two parties to trade a security or currency at a specified price and date.

Futures: Like forward contracts, but traded on an exchange. Futures are typically settled in cash, rather than requiring delivery of a security or currency. Best known: S&P 500 futures.

Gamma: The rate at which delta moves up or down in response to changes in the price of the underlying.

Options: A "call" option allows you to buy a security at a set time for a set price; a "put" option gives you a similar right to sell a security.

Put: An option giving the holder the right, but not the obligation, to sell a specific quantity of an asset for a fixed price during a specific period.

RHO: The rate at which the price of an option changes in response to a given move in interest rates.

Structured Notes: Corporate or government debt instruments created by dealers in which the interest rate or principal is pegged to an unrelated indicator: the price of oil, the Nikkei index, etc.

Swaps: Most common are interest rate swaps, where two parties exchange interest rate payments on a common principal: floating for fixed rate, or one currency for another. If a manager who owned a floating-rate note were convinced interest rates were going to fall, he might want to enter into a swap in order to get fixed-rate payments instead. Equity swaps are growing in popularity.

Swaption: An option giving the holder the right to enter into or cancel a swap at a future date.

Theta: The rate at which the price of an option changes because of the passage of time. Also known as "time decay."

Underlying: The asset, reference rate or index whose price movement determines the value of the derivative.

Vega: The rate at which the price of an option changes because of a change in the volatility of the underlying.

How Derivatives Work

As the volatility of financial markets has increased recently, analysts have pointed to many causes. One is the big bets being made by hedge funds. Another is the impact of derivatives, which are specially designed investments that are linked to the performance of an underlying asset, like a stock, or the performance of a financial market, like interest rates in the bond market. Many hedge funds have used derivatives aggressively but they can also be employed by smaller investors and can assist companies in offsetting the risk of changes in currency and interest rate markets. Some of these derivatives can be so complex that even the people who design them are not completely sure of the risks involved, either for the buyer or the seller. Following are examples of some simple derivatives, in which risk is transferred from buyers to sellers for a fee and often because they have different market outlooks.

An Interest-Rate Cap

What It Is: An arrangement that pays the buyer a set amount if interest rates rise above a set level.

Who Might Buy One: A life insurance company.

Why: When interest rates rise, policyholders are apt to exercise their right to borrow from their insurance policies at low rates.

In the early 1980s, for example, when interest rates were at double-digit levels, tens of thousands of customers exercised the right to borrow at single-digit rates guaranteed by their policies. This allowed the customers to borrow money at low rates and reinvest it at higher rates for a profit. But it was costly to insurers because they were lending at lower-than-prevailing rates. An interest-rate cap can offset an insurer's costs in making these lower-rate loans.

The Buyer's Risk: Paying for nothing. If rates do not rise, the interest-rate cap would not kick in and the insurer would be out the cost of buying the cap.

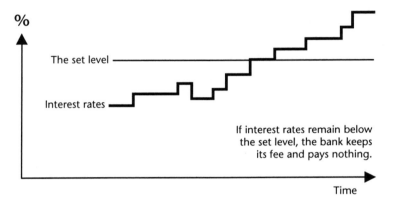

IF THE BUYER IS RIGHT and interest rates rise above the set level, the seller of the cap will pay the agreed-upon amount, which the insurer will use to offset the amount it is losing by lending money at lower rates.

Figure 2.8: If the Buyer Is Right

Who Would Sell One: A bank.

Why: To collect a fee. If the rates fail to rise, the bank keeps the fee and pays nothing.

The Seller's Risk: If the rates rise, the bank pays the insurer the agreed-upon amount, which is only partially offset by the fee.

A Put Contract on the Futures Market

What It Is: A contract to sell a commodity at a set price on a certain day, regardless of the market price available that day.

Who Might Buy One: A farmer with 200 acres of corn that he wants to sell.

Why: To lock in a price that covers the farmer's costs and allows ample profit. With an agreement in place, the farmer no longer needs to worry about what price he will get for his crop when the corn is harvested.

The Buyer's Risk: If the market price rises and is higher than the agreed-upon price on the day of the grain sale, the farmer still must sell for the lower, agreed-upon price.

IF THE FARMER IS RIGHT and market prices fall, the food company that agreed to buy the farmer's corn will have to buy it at higher-than-market rates. As long as the cost of the contract is less than the price disparity, the farmer will come out ahead.

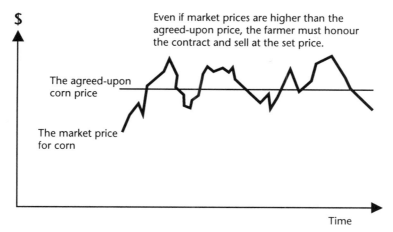

Figure 2.9: If the Farmer Is Right

Who Would Sell One: A food company that needs corn.

Why: To lock in a price and collect a fee. If the market price rises, the food company can buy corn at a lower-than-market price.

The Seller's Risk: Even if corn is available on the market at lower prices that day, the food company is committed to buying from the farmer at the agreed-upon price. The fee paid by the farmer may not fully offset the difference between the agreed-upon price and the market price, meaning the food company paid more than necessary for the corn it needed.

An Interest-Rate Swap

What It Is: An agreement between two companies that enables a company that has taken out a floating-rate loan to pay a fixed interest rate.

Who Might Buy One: Company A that borrowed money at a floating interest rate — for example the prime plus one percentage point — but is worried that rates might rise.

Why: Company A needs money now, but is worried that if interest rates rise it may not be able to afford the higher payments.

The Risk to Company A: After the swap is set, interest rates may fall but the company would still be obligated to pay the higher, fixed rate.

Who Would Sell One: Company B, which is willing to pay floating rates.

Why: Company B believes the floating rate will fall and it will pay rates that are less than the fixed rate it receives from Company A.

The Risk to Company B: If rates rise, Company B would end up paying interest rates that are higher than the fixed interest rate it receives from Company A.

Who Wins? Company A gets the rate it wanted. Company B's success depends on how rates move.

How It Works
Company A swaps interest rates with Company B

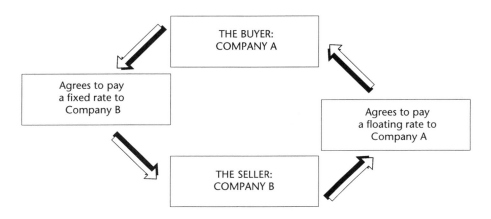

Figure 2.10: How an Interest-Rate Swap Works

Some Guidelines to Follow

In light of the recent volatility in interest rates, the stock markets, mortgage rates, bond prices, and Canadian currency, it is imperative that you establish certain rules to protect yourself against imprudent investments.

"The road to financial insecurity is paved with good intentions" is one of this author's basic financial laws. The points below are for the Conservative Investor.

1) Know the upside and downside of every investment before you act. Do not buy any investment unless you know exactly how much you stand to lose if it fails. Learn to be comfortable with the degree of risk that is acceptable to you. Betting on commodities, futures or high-risk stocks is not appropriate for most people.

2) Make sure your portfolio has the proper degree of diversification, and learn to adapt that diversification to changing market conditions. Divide your money between real estate, stocks, bonds and cash. The younger you are, the more

risk you can tolerate. Adjust the equity portion of your holdings downward as interest rates rise. Do not get caught in pseudo diversification where you believe you are diversified because you have five mutual funds. If it consists of five equity funds, then it is not diversification. You need equity bond and money market funds to be diversified.

3) Avoid all opportunities that are so hot that you must act "now" to get in on the ground floor. People are attracted to new offerings, new products and new multilevel marketing systems. Most look good on paper, most will fail. Cool off and wait to see how the "new" concepts do after awhile. You may miss the old real opportunity but you will still have your money intact.

4) Don't let the fear of taxation determine your investment choices. Choose what is appropriate for your risk preference and experience. The one thing worse than paying income tax is to have no income to tax at all. Many deals — film tax shelters, limited partnerships, oil and gas partnerships — have failed in the past. It must first be a good investment even if it has tax consequences. Many people go to extremes to save taxes and lose the profit on their investments as a result.

5) Part of making a profit is learning when to take a profit. The essence is to know when to sell. Don't be motivated by greed, looking for 100 per cent returns; 20 per cent is very nice if you take it.

6) Carefully monitor your investments. Check to see how you are doing. Use the latest software. Some of the best purely Canadian financial software are *Wealth Creator and Portfolio Tracker* from RAM Technologies at (905) 795-9222; and *Bell Charts* on mutual funds at (416) 515-4757. These will assist you in determining when to buy or sell or change your investment strategies. They are inexpensive and put you in control of your financial future.

CHAPTER THREE

Equities

Whether the Conservative Investor likes it or not, you cannot obtain meaningful returns on investment without a component of equities in your portfolio. A minimum threshold of 25 per cent equities is essential for even the oldest investor. Equity selection is both an art and a science, and as our goals are to reduce risk and preserve capital, we must learn to find approaches that allow us to learn to achieve both and which are also simple to follow.

Most investors want some simple magic — perhaps software or an all-knowing guru. I personally believe this is abdicating personal responsibility. We must understand what we are buying and why. Our broker or financial planner can help us and give us the benefit of their knowledge and experience, but unless we understand the market and risk, we are bound to make errors.

There is much conflict about stock markets and where they are going. Oil prices are rising while gold is stable. Interest rates are up and volatile despite the fact that there is no real inflation. In the U.S., the Federal Reserve Board is affecting nearly all world markets because of its fear of rapid growth and potential inflation. Corporate profits and productivity are soaring, and North American firms are more competitive than ever.

Canada is being downgraded because of our massive deficits and national unity concerns. Eastern Europe and Russia are in a mess. The markets seem to overreact to any bad news and inadequately respond to good news, and there has been a massive inflow of funds into the market from mutual funds, yet the market performance has been only so-so.

Mutual fund companies now control about 10 per cent of the Canadian and American equity markets. Consumers such as yourself still control about 50 per cent, and the rest is held by institutional investors such as pension funds, insurance companies and foreign corporations.

THE COMPONENTS OF UNDERSTANDING THE MARKET

Extending our principles of asset allocation and diversification, the average Conservative Investor will need 25 per cent to 45 per cent of their portfolio in various forms of equities, and eight to 15 different equities and equity mutual funds to be properly diversified.

Should we select large blue chip stocks — those that pay dividends, small growth companies, international stocks or growth and income mutual funds?

Table 3.1

HOW MARKETS RANK: ESTIMATED STOCK MARKET CAPITALIZATION, IN BILLIONS ($U.S.)	
United States	$4,467
Japan	2,885
Britain	1,190
France	453
Germany	442
Hong Kong	380
Switzerland	250
Canada	230
Malaysia	230
Mexico	201

We will deal with international investing strategies and mutual fund analysis in later chapters, but the groundwork for conservative decision-making which began in the previous chapter is a collection of building blocks of cumulative understanding and comprehension to reduce the emotionalism of decision-making and to make rational choices.

THINGS CHANGE

The investment world of the 1990s is dramatically different from the 1960s, '70s and '80s, while 70 per cent of the market is still large blue chip companies.

Figure 3.1

THE DOW JONES INDUSTRIAL AVERAGE, THEN AND NOW

1950	1994
Allied Chemical	Allied Signal
American Can	Alcoa
American Smelting	American Express
American Telephone & Telegraph	American Telephone & Telegraph
American Tobacco B	Bethlehem Steel
Bethlehem Steel	Boeing
Chrysler	Caterpillar
Coca-Cola	Chevron
Corn Products Refining	Coca-Cola
DuPont	Disney
Eastman Kodak	DuPont
General Electric	Eastman Kodak
General Foods	Exxon
General Motors	General Electric
Goodyear	General Motors
International Harvester	Goodyear
International Nickel	IBM
Johns-Manville	International Paper
Loew's	McDonald's
National Distiller	Merck
National Steel	Minnesota Mining & Manufacturing
Procter & Gamble	Morgan (J.P.)
Standard Oil (CA)	Philip Morris
Standard Oil (NJ)	Procter & Gamble
Texas Corp.	Sears
Union Carbide	Texaco
United Aircraft	Union Carbide
U.S. Steel	United Technologies
Westinghouse Electric	Westinghouse Electric
Woolworth	Woolworth

Smaller companies are having a greater impact as are more foreign ones. Figure 3.1 shows the 1950 and 1994 makeup of the Dow Jones Industrial Average 30 which was first created in 1928.

In the 1950s, the list was mainly oils, metals and heavy equipment. Only 16 companies from 1950 are with us today.

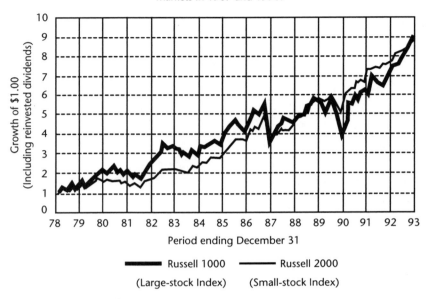

Figure 3.2: Large Stocks vs. Small Stocks

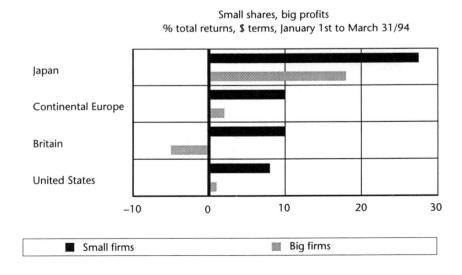

Figure 3.3: Small Shares, Big Profits

40

Table 3.2: Listing Rules

Exchange	Listing fee for foreign company	Minimum offering ($ millions)	Minimum # of noninsider shareholders	Minimum profitability period (yrs)	Minimum pre-tax income
Asian Board (Van.)	$2,400	1.8	300	2	$288,000
NASDAQ	$7,500–$50,000	3–15	400–800	1–2	$750,000
Toronto SE	Up to $18,000	7	3,000	3	$1.44m
NYSE	$100,000	18	5,000	3	$100m

The Toronto Stock Exchange (TSE) is the world's sixth most important exchange. More and more Canadian companies are listed on exchanges in the U.S. and soon even in Europe, while many new Chinese companies are listing in Vancouver.

I have no personal bias against the Vancouver Exchange. Many of the small mining and speculative penny stocks I grew up with in the 1960s in Toronto moved West. It's a place of fun and excitement, and a home for new companies and dynamic promoters. Many companies are good risks and start in Vancouver, and then move east to Toronto or NASDAQ as they grow. But there are bad deals as well, and it's generally not for the Conservative Investor.

Vancouver is opening a new Asian listing board for Hong Kong and Far East promoters. It will be a place for companies from the Pacific Rim that can't get listed out there. As you'll see from the listing fee chart, it will be a cheap and easy listing. I would tread carefully about this once again.

Over the last 30 years, I have been in equity markets. I have learned what economic indicators are the best general forecasters of stock market trends. Will we go into a declining (bear) or rising (bull) market, and for how long is a primary equity a selection factor? This will affect our portfolio weighing.

Obviously, if the fundamentals show a clear downward trend, we need to reduce our holdings by, say, 10 per cent to 15 per cent and get into more stable investments. Or if the trend is for substantial growth, we should reduce our cash and enhance our equity holdings, remembering that at least 70 per cent of our equity and equity-based mutual funds are for a long-term hold.

THE FUNDAMENTALS — HOW TO EVALUATE THE MARKET TRENDS

What we want are indicators that will show us enough about the market's valuation, the direction of interest rates and the general health of the economy in unison to allow us to understand trends. The approach can be adapted for the U.S. market and foreign markets as well.

Market Valuation

Start With: The TSE 300 dividend yield for the previous four quarters.

To Get It: Contact Info Globe Services or the TSE or your broker/planner.

What It Means: If yields are 3.5 per cent or less and falling, the signal is negative. If over 4.5 per cent and rising, the signal is positive and the market is rising.
For the U.S., use the Standard & Poor's 500 Dividend Yield.

Comparing Earnings and Fixed-Income Securities

When returns are poor on GICs and bonds, the stock generally attracts a lot of money.

Start With: The Price/Earnings Ratio for the TSE 300 based on the previous four quarters and the current three-month Treasury Bill rate.

To Get Them: *The Globe and Mail's Report on Business, The Financial Times* or *The Financial Post.* Also your broker or planner.

The Calculation:

1) Start with the P/E Ratio   _____

2) Divide #1 by itself, the square root   _____

3) Multiply #2 by 100   _____

4) Enter the current 3 month T-Bill rate   _____

5) Subtract #4 from #3   _____

What It Means: If line #5 is positive — say 1 to 1.5 or better — the general market value is reasonable. If it is negative, the market will trend down as GIC holders will dump stocks and buy more security and less risk. A 1 per cent rise in interest rates over 6 per cent reduces consumer stock holdings by as much as 10 per cent.

Bank of Canada Rate Changes

This is the most significant domestic factor affecting stock market trends. In the U.S., it is the Federal Reserve Rate. This dominates all trends. The plateau is in the 25 per cent to 26 per cent range. If the increases are in excess of 25 per cent, then the increases will probably plateau and come down. If they are less than 25 per cent, they will continue to rise and the market will continue to decline.

Start with the Bank of Canada Rate: This week, a month ago, and 16 months ago and 18 months ago.

To Get Them: Contact Statistics Canada, Info Globe or The Bank of Canada.

The Calculation:

1) The rate from 30 days ago   ————————————

2) The rate from 18 months ago   ————————————

3) Divide #1 by #2   ————————————

4) Subtract #1 from #3   ————————————

5) Multiply #4 by 100   ————————————

6) This week's rate   ————————————

7) The rate 16 months ago   ————————————

8) Divide #6 by #7   ————————————

9) Deduct #1 from #8   ————————————

10) Multiply #9 by 100   ————————————

Compare lines 5 and 10: If line 5 is negative and less than -5, and if line 10 is negative and greater than -5, the indication is downward for the market. If line 5 is positive and greater than 25, and line 10 is positive and less than 25, the sign is positive for money coming into the market.

Magnitude of Increase: If the prime rate charged by retail banks to their customers for short-term loans is rising, the market is likely to trend downwards. The market can still move upwards despite upward interest rates. Therefore, the magnitude of the increase is what we have to consider as well as the rate of increase.

Start With: The current bank prime rate as well as the peak prime rate the last 12 months and its previous bottom position over the past 12 months.

To Get Them: Most are listed in daily newspapers. Call your local bank for information.

The Calculation:

1) If the rate has been rising for the most recent low, enter the low. If it is declining for the most recent high, enter the high.   _____

2) Enter the current prime rate   _____

3) Divide #2 by #1   _____

4) Deduct 1 from #3   _____

5) Multiply #4 from 100   _____

What It Means: If rates are rising and #5 is 8 or more, it's bad news. If rates are falling and #5 is 4.5 or more, it's a positive sign for stocks.

The Economy: Industrial Activity

If manufacturing and industrial production is on the rise, the trend is positive. This is a measure of economic strength. If growth is excessive — say, over 3.5 per cent to 4 per cent — then there may be a threat of inflation and the market will trend down.

Start With: The rate of industrial production today and 12 months ago.

To Get Them: Contact Statistics Canada or your bank or brokerage research department.

The Calculation:

1) Today's rate of industrial production   _____

2) The rate from 12 months ago   _____

3) Divide #1 by #2   _____

4) Subtract 1 from #3   _____

5) Multiply #4 by 100   _____

If #5 is higher than 6, the trend is negative as the market may be overheated. If it is less than 4, the sign is a good one.

These ratios are aggregates and, at times, may be neutral or possibly contrary. If neutral, the assumption is generally positive. If there are contradictory numbers, the trend is usually dominated by the interest rate numbers.

THE QUEST FOR LOWER RISK THROUGH VALUE

I mentioned previously that value and not risk is a better indicator of equity growth. I remember reading in 1976 the works of the late Ben Graham who wrote the first book, *Security Analysis*, that highlighted the real benefit of value analysis and investing. Graham's models have equal validity if we see a positive equity climate.

I like Ben Graham because he was a true conservative. He wanted bargains but he also wanted rock-solid assets, so he looked at risk and reward. Graham analyzed annual reports using 10 basic questions. They are just as invaluable nearly 20 years later.

Measures of Risk

1) Is the 10-year average earnings per share growth rate greater than 7 per cent?

2) Is total debt for the company less than twice net current assets?

3) Are current assets more than twice current liabilities?

4) Is the debt-to-equity ratio less than 1?

5) Were there no more than two years out of 10 with earnings declines greater than 5 per cent?

Measures of Reward

1) Is the stock market price less than two-thirds of net current assets?

2) Is the stock market price less than two-thirds of the book value?

3) Is the price/earnings less than 40 per cent of the average price/earnings over the past five years?

4) Is the price/earnings less than half the reciprocal of the yield of a triple A-rated corporate bond?

5) Is the dividend yield more than two-thirds the yield of a triple A-rated corporate bond yield?

What's great about all of these calculations is that they can all be done on the computer in seconds.

ANOTHER OPTION — DIVIDENDS TO REDUCE RISK

With the growing uncertainty and volatility of interest rates and bond funds being less than stellar, what other options in equities are open to the Conservative Investor?

The best one is to buy quality stocks with high-dividend payouts or equity-income funds made up of portfolios of these shares.

We have also seen the quality yields of stocks such as the Bank of Nova Scotia, BCE and BC Tel. These pay generous dividends with yields of 4.5 per cent to 6.5 per cent. As dividends from Canadian sources are substantially tax ameliorated by the dividend tax credit, the return is even greater. Depending on your marginal tax rate, the return is multiplied by 1.25 per cent to 1.28 per cent to get the interest income equivalent in terms of pre-tax cash flow.

Canadian source dividends have generally outpaced the rate of inflation. Especially as our goal is long-term asset appreciation and capital preservation, you will not experience the concerns of daily fluctuations in stock market prices. Steady dividend increases impact on stock prices by enhancing capital appreciation. For early retirees or those age 60 to 70, in good health, you'll want some dividend-income producers in your portfolio because of the regularized cash flow and lower risk.

The current yield, which is the annual payout dividend divided by the market price of one share, is rising for many blue chip Canadian stocks as prices in the market have slipped back.

I strongly recommend companies that have raised dividends 5 per cent annually over the past 10 years and those with strong earnings growth. There are usually mature companies with strong capitalization including major utilities, banks and oil companies. The dividend tax credit is the gravy on top of the return.

DIVIDEND REINVESTMENT PLANS (DRIPS)

My friend Dale Ennis, editor and publisher of the *Canadian Moneysaver* (one of my all-time favourite monthly publications that every Conservative Investor should subscribe to), is madly in love with DRIPs. Figure 3.4 lists of the best Canadian and American DRIPs.

Figure 3.4: The Best Canadian and American DRIPs

COMPANY	INDUSTRY	ANNUAL DIVIDEND GROWTH RATE	NO. OF YEARS INCREASED	CASH INVESTMENTS/ FREQUENCY
Abbott Laboratories	health care products	18.9%	20	$10-$5,000/quarter
AFLAC	insurance	17.5	10	$20-$5,000/month
American Business Products	business supplies and books	13.4	35	$10-$1,000/month
American Recreation Centers*	bowling alleys, direct marketing	13.0	25	$25-$5,000/month
Anheuser-Busch Co.	brewing	18.0	18	$25-$5,000/month
Avery Dennison Corp.	stationery and office products	13.8	17	$25-$3,000/month
C.R. Bard	health care products	19.1	21	$10-$2,500/month
Baxter International	health care products	14.2	36	$25-$25,000/year
Clorox Co.	consumer products	13.9	16	$10-$60,000/year#

COMPANY	INDUSTRY	ANNUAL DIVIDEND GROWTH RATE	NO. OF YEARS INCREASED	CASH INVESTMENTS/ FREQUENCY
ConAgra	food processing	15.5	15	$25-$5,000/quarter
Crompton & Knowles Corp.	dyes, flavors, colors, fragrances	14.9	16	$30-$3,000/quarter
Dean Foods+	dairy and specialty foods	15.6	20	$25-$3,000/quarter
Fifth Third Bancorp	bank holding company	15.1	20	$25-$1,000/month
Flowers Industries	packaged foods	15.7	20	$25-$3,000/month
General Mills Products	packaged foods, restaurants	13.8	28	$10-$3,000/quarter#
Giant Food	supermarkets	17.8	12	$10-$1,000/quarter
Golden Enterprises	food, bolt fasteners	15.0	15	No cash investments
Hannaford Brothers Co.	retail food and drugs	14.9	21	$25-$2,000/month
Harcourt General	publishing, specialty retailing	15.8	25	$25-$2,500/quarter
John H. Harland Co.	checks, financial stationery	19.2	40	$25-$3,000/quarter
Hartford Steam Boiler	boiler and machinery insurance	19.2	27	$10-$1,000/month
H.J. Heinz Co.	processed food products	16.2	29	$25-$5,000/month
Johnson & Johnson	health care products	13.9	30	$25-$50,000/year#
Luby's Cafeterias	cafeterias	14.1	19	$20-$5,000/quarter#
Nucor Corp.	steel products	13.4	20	$10-$3,000/quarter
Pall Corp.	filters	17.8	12	$10-$5,000/month
Pep Boys	retail auto-parts stores	13.2	15	$100-$10,000/quarter
Philip Morris Cos.	tobacco, consumer products	22.7	24	$10-$60,000/year#
Quaker Oats Co.	foods, beverages, pet food	14.4	26	$10-$3,000/year
RPM	protective coatings	15.0	19	$25-$5,000/month§
Rite Aid Corp.	retail drugstores	15.2	24	$25-$25,000/year#
Rubbermaid	plastic, rubber products	16.1	38	$10-$3,000/quarter
Sara Lee Corp.	food and consumer products	16.5	16	$10-$5,000/quarter
ServiceMaster LP	management services	15.9	22	$25-$25,000/month
Sherwin-Williams Co.	paints, varnishes, coatings	13.4	13	$10-$2,000/month
J.M. Smucker Co.	jams, jellies	18.5	17	$20-$1,500/month
Sysco Corp.	food and related products distrib.	21.0	16	No cash investments
UST	smokeless tobacco products	17.8	22	$10-$10,000/month§
Wachovia Corp.	interstate bank holding company	14.1	15	$20-$2,000/month
Wilmington Trust Corp.	banking and related services	17.3	11	$10-$5,000/quarter
Wm. Wrigley Jr. Co.	chewing gum	16.9	12	$50-$5,000/month

*$100 initial payment if not shareholder. +Must have at least 25 shares to join DRIP.

#Cash can be invested monthly. §Cash can be invested twice a month.

Figure 3.5: Canadian Dividend Reinvestment Plans

COMMON STOCKS WITH BOTH DIVIDEND REINVESTMENT PLANS AND SHARE PURCHASE PLANS

STOCK – SYMBOL	52 WEEK HIGH $	52 WEEK LOW $	DIVIDEND $	RECENT PRICE	YIELD %
Alberta Energy - AEC	23.67	15.50	0.35	18.25	1.9
Alcan – AL	29.67	21.67	0.30	28.87	1.0
BC Gas– BCG	17.00	15.12	0.90	16.75	5.4
BC Telecom - BCT	26.00	18.67	1.20	25.12	4.8
BCE Inc – BCE	47.00	40.75	2.68	45.00	5.9
Bank of Montreal – BMO	28.00	21.37	1.12	27.67	4.1
Bank of Nova Scotia – BNS	30.75	21.87	1.16	30.67	3.8
Bruncor – BRR	24.50	18.75	1.28	24.50	5.2
Canadian Pacific – CP	23.12	15.87	0.32	21.87	1.5
Cdn Imperial Bank (CIBC) – CM	33.67	23.67	1.32	32.87	4.0
Dofasco – DFS	24.25	9.50	0.00	24.00	0.0
Fortis – FTS	29.25	23.50	1.60	28.37	5.7
General Motors – GM	75.75	42.50	0.80	75.37	1.1
Imasco – IMS	41.12	34.25	1.48	40.67	3.6
Imperial Oil – IMO	50.25	42.12	1.80	45.37	4.0
Inco – N	37.00	23.12	0.40	35.87	1.1
Island Tel – IT	25.75	17.50	1.20	25.50	4.7
MDS Health 'A' – MHG.A	18.00	11.50	0.12	13.00	0.9
Maritime T & T – MTT	25.75	18.87	1.24	24.37	5.1
National Bank – NA	11.12	7.25	0.40	10.50	3.8
Newtel Ent – NEL	24.25	18.37	1.36	23.67	5.8
Northern Telecom – NTL	58.37	27.50	0.36	43.25	**
Nova – NVA	10.12	8.37	0.24	9.50	2.5
TransAlta Util – TA	15.50	12.67	0.98	15.12	6.5
TransCanada Pipeline (TCPL) – TRP	21.87	16.12	0.92	19.75	4.7

To calculate yield, divide the dividend by the current price. The pre-tax interest yield compares to dividend yield by 1.32% (e.g., Canada Savings Bonds of 6% = 6% divided by 1.32 = 4.55 dividend yield). This 1.32 equivalent yield factor is for top–bracket taxpayers in Ontario, BC, and SK. Residents of AB and PQ use 1.28; NB, NF, NS and PE use 1.33; MB uses 1.29; NT and YK use 1.26. ** Dividend in $U.S.

Sample minimum and maximum investments are generally $50 minimum purchase and $20,000 maximum at little or no fee and up to 5 per cent discount.

If you decide to own them, buy at least one share and have it registered in your name. The owner or your spouse or children qualifies to have the dividends reinvested to purchase future shares from the company at little or no fee. Some share purchase plans let you buy shares at discounts of up to 5 per cent and this, of course, reduces your cost of investing and enhances your return.

There are 85 Canadian and 850 American firms who do the same.

Each quarter you reinvest the dividends and grow your equity. Many DRIPs let you buy more shares for cash at the same time you bypass your broker commission as well.

LOWER COSTS EQUAL HIGHER RETURNS

As with the DRIPs above, the low cost or discount adds to your returns and lowers risk. As you get progressively more sophisticated, you should be able to conduct your equity trades through discount brokers. Many financial–planning firms use them as their "back room" for clearing purposes and offer the discount broker rates on all equity trades.

Obviously, low costs mean more money to invest and better capital deployment. There are also clearly times when we are penny wise and pound foolish.

At least 50 per cent or more of the population need financial advice and direction. For most, an independent financial planner working with a good independent insurance agent is ideal. At least 30 per cent of the population are better off using a full–service brokerage firm. They are particularly good at sending out reports and research as well as servicing high-net-worth customers with excellent international services.

Discount brokers offer real value and no frills. Firms such as Green Line now have over 500,000 customers and obviously they are doing something right.

You have to select your comfort level and need for service.

Figure 3.6: Discount Brokers

| | CANADIAN STOCKS | | | MUTUAL FUNDS | |
	$1	$20	$40	FEES FOR TRADES LESS THAN $2,000	FRONT-END LOAD
TD Bank's Green Line	$40 and 0.5¢	$40 and 0.5¢	$40 and 0.7¢	$45	$1,000–$4,999: 2.5% $5,000–$24,999: 2% $25,000 and up: 1%
CIBC's Investors Edge	$40 and 0.5¢	$40 and 0.5¢	$40 and 0.7¢	$45	Up to $5,000: 2.5% $5,001–$24,999: 2% $25,000 and up: 1%
Royal Bank's Action Direct	$35 and 0.1¢	$35 and 0.5¢	$35 and 0.7¢	$40	$2,000–$24,999: 2% $25,000 and up: 1%
Bank of Montreal's Investor Line	$25 and 0.5¢	$25 and 0.4¢	$25 and 0.6¢	$25	Up to $25,000: 2% $25,000 and up: 1% Min. commission: $100
Scotiabank's Scotia Discount Brokerage	$25 and 0.5¢	$25 and 0.4¢	$25 and 0.6¢	$25	Up to $25,000: 2% $25,000 and up: 1% Min. commission: $50
Mouvement Desjardin's Disnat (Quebec only)	$35 and 0.5¢	$25 and 4.5¢	$35 and 6.5¢	$45	Up to $25,000: 2% $25,000 and up: Negotiable Min. commission: $45

SMALL STOCKS AND SMALL CAPS

Is it inconsistent to invest in the more exciting performance of small stocks and small cap mutual funds and still be a low–risk Conservative Investor?

Well, let's look at the real numbers. Historically, small stocks have outperformed larger ones over the last 40 years by a yearly average of 4 per cent. Small companies are generally on the leading edge of a recovery outperforming the big ones when the economy is on an upswing and dropping more sharply in a downturn.

Small stocks rely more heavily on borrowing than larger ones. As a result, their stocks are particularly sensitive to improved cash flows, which makes it easier for them to service their debts. When interest rates tumble, small caps get a big boost.

As they are generally in the fast–growing areas of the economy, they lead the market. Yet despite the central tenet of efficient–market theory espoused by most graduate business schools — that investors can consistently earn higher returns only by taking bigger risks — recent research shows that small stocks were not in themselves inherently riskier than bigger ones.

Following this advice resulted in seven years of nonperformance between 1985 and 1992. Many mutual funds and pension managers dumped small stocks to buy market indexes instead, especially because the takeover and merger and acquisition business took off again in 1992–1993.

Small stocks are less liquid and more volatile, and can fail. They are best purchased only by those under 50 who want a 5 per cent hedge and no more. They are wrong for the Conservative Investor over age 60.

CHAPTER FOUR

Mutual Funds

There is a massive transformation of the investment at work in Canada. It started in 1989 with the decline in interest rates. Tens of billions of dollars moved from GICs and bonds to mutual funds, and the industry grew 400 per cent in five years.

The same period saw an increase from fewer than 500 funds to nearly 800. By January 1994, $2 billion a month was moving out of bank deposits, and the industry passed the $100-billion mark. Many forecast it will reach $400 billion by the end of the decade.

Canadians held $500 billion in bank deposits and $250 billion in Canada Savings Bonds and GICs in 1992. But the shift is on.

The problem is that many novice and elderly investors impacted by the sticker shock of the low interest rates chose to move money into products they didn't understand and without an overall strategy. The result is perhaps a serious fiscal disaster in the making.

In the early part of 1994, with all markets except Western Europe trailing down, there were few redemptions until interest rates rose. Since more than half of the investments went to banks, they were eager to keep savings rates low and retain the mutual fund dollars. But by April the investor, convinced that a mutual fund is a speculative equity buy and not a long-term hold, began redemptions at $1.5 billion a month. Error is being built on error.

People are buying mutual funds — or more correctly, are being sold mutual funds — instead of making strategic investments. They lack diversification. They don't understand volatility and risk, and they invest by the trend or the hot hand and not where the market is going.

They are further misled and ill-served by a proliferation of mutual funds books on picks using six-month-old data written by journalists from newspapers who have never earned more than $50,000 a year in their life and who have no real background or qualification in securities strategy. Some writers are simply touts for some funds and shills to draw in the "great unwashed."

Exceptions to this are Stephen Gadsden's book, *The Canadian Consumer's Guide to Mutual Funds*, which explains strategy and asset allocation for Canadians; John Boggle, founder of the giant Vanguard Funds in the U.S., who wrote *John Boggle on Mutual Funds*; and Steven Kelman's *1994 Mutual Fund Guide*.

In New York, I got to hear investment analyst Don Christensen, who has written the proverbial armaggedonist book entitled *Surviving the Coming Mutual Fund Crisis*. He sees a 1929 collapse even though the leverage is not in the market, regulation is tight and the economy is under stricter control. Since 1990, Christensen has warned that many funds following high-risk policies of buying shares in small, new companies, concentrating their portfolio in narrow sectors and owning shares that are illiquid, are beginning to creep back.

Funds are also using options and derivatives. Christensen says we need to be worried about all of this. He warns against buying stock funds with yearly expenses exceeding 1.25 per cent and any other high-expense funds above group norms.

Many writers and experts agree with him that annual reports and prospectuses are less than forthcoming and downplay losses and poor performance.

More and more funds are team managed — nearly 30 per cent. The investor must know who manages their money. Analysts agree that it is imperative to avoid funds that lead the short-term performance charts as they are too risky.

I like mutual funds and most mutual fund industry people. Mutual funds have been good to Canadians. They have professional management, offer diversification, allow for small investments, provide liquidity usually in five business days, and provide low-cost services to investors.

Mutual funds should be highly represented in your portfolio with a permanent component of RRSPs, and RRIFs as well.

In writing this chapter, I assume you know what a mutual fund is and the most basic types that are available and how to buy them. For those who have questions, may I refer you to *Strategic Personal Investing: Gold Edition* (Toronto: Warwick 1994), which contains a detailed explanation of the options and alternatives here.

This chapter is about mutual funds fact and fiction as well as strategies and tactics for mutual fund investing and the latest research in the field.

We should tend to look at the three and five year numbers. Avoid all funds in the bottom 10 per cent of performance and especially the ones using terms such as "high yield" or "high income." It simply means, "high risk."

Figure 4.1: How to Read a Mutual Fund Table

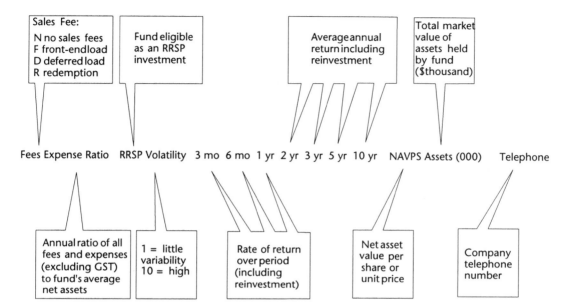

Table 4.1: Mutual Fund Performance after the Crunch at May 1994

ONE-YEAR WINNERS	1 YEAR	1 MONTH
1. ABC Fundamental-Value	80.59%	.26%
2. Goldfund Ltd.	73.03%	−6.67%
3. Multiple Opportunities	63.27%	−10.00%
4. BPI Global Small Companies	63.25%	.44%
5. Dynamic Precious Metals	59.57%	−4.66%
6. ABC Fully-Managed	48.91%	.04%
7. Investors Pacific International	47.96%	3.46%
8. Goldtrust	47.81%	−6.67%
9. Hyperion Asian Trust	46.47%	3.98%
10. Templeton Emerging Markets	46.32%	−4.90%

THREE-YEAR WINNERS	3 YEAR	1 MONTH
1. Marathon Equity	50.40%	1.73%
2. Altamira Resource	44.55%	.93%

3. Prudential Natural Resource	36.56%	1.25%
4. ABC Fundamental-Value	36.27%	.26%
5. Multiple Opportunities	35.81%	−10.00%
6. Dynamic Canadian Growth	35.68%	−.58%
7. Universal Canadian Resource	34.68%	1.65%
8. Altamira Equity	32.90%	−.73%
9. BT Landmark Resource	32.09%	−1.24%
10. Dominion Equity Resource	32.06%	6.39%

FIVE-YEAR WINNERS	5 YEAR	1 MONTH
1. ABC Fundamental-Value	28.84%	.26%
2. Altamira Equity	26.84%	−.73%
3. Marathon Equity	25.91%	−1.73%
4. Multiple Opportunities	23.58%	−10.00%
5. Bullock American	23.39%	−4.15%
6. Dynamic Canadian Growth	22.11%	−.58%
7. Prudential Natural Resource	21.83%	1.25%
8. GBC Canadian Growth	20.02%	−.60%
9. Altamira Special Growth	19.93%	−3.40%
10. BPI American Equity Growth	19.68%	−2.54%

OVER 10 YEARS	PERCENT RETURN	VALUE
1. C.I. Pacific Fund	19.40%	5,888
2. Bullock American Fund	18.22%	5,330
3. Trimark Fund	16.56%	4,628
4. Cambridge Growth Fund (Sagit Mgnt)	16.35%	4,544
5. MD Growth Investments Ltd.	15.87%	4,364
6. Templeton Growth Fund Ltd.	15.24%	4,132
7. Canada Life U.S. & Int. Equity S-34	15.08%	4,074
8. Imperial Growth Canadian Equity	14.83%	3,985
9. General Trust of Canada U.S. Equity	14.55%	3,891
10. Philips, Hager & North U.S. Equity	14.27%	3,797

Table 4.2: How the Large Funds Fared

The 15 largest mutual funds in Canada and their returns from February 1 to April 30, 1994

FUND	TYPE	TOTAL NET ASSETS ($ MILLION)	3-MONTH RETURN (%)
Investors Mortgage Fund	Mortgage	$3,574	–4.01%
First Canadian Mortgage Fund	Mortgage	2,700	–4.26
Investors Dividend Fund	Dividend	2,586	–5.31
Templeton Growth Fund Ltd.	Int'l Equity	2,380	–1.70
Green Line Canadian Money Mkt.	Money Mkt.	2,226	+0.92
Royfund Balanced Fund	Balanced	2,207	–3.95
First Canadian Money Market	Money Mkt.	1,950	+0.78
Royfund Canadian T-Bill Fund	Money Mkt.	1,906	+0.80
Industrial Income Fund (Mackenzie)	Balanced	1,897	–7.70
Trimark RSP Equity Fund	Cdn. Equity	1,816	–4.42
CIBC Mortgage Investment Fund	Mortgage	1,802	–3.47
Royfund Mortgage Fund	Mortgage	1,755	–2.81
Fidelity Far East Fund	Int'l Equity	1,720	–12.38
Investors Bond Fund	Bond	1,706	–7.86
Altamira Equity Fund	Cdn. Equity	1,672	–3.41

Source: Globe Information Services

Figure 4.2: Canadian Equity Style Grid

Core funds are those in the upper left section of the grid. They are lower risk and perform well in down markets. Funds toward the lower right section are specialty or non-core holdings. They will complement a foundation of core holdings especially given their strong performance potential in up markets. Hold funds from different boxes to diversify by style.

	VALUE		BLEND	GROWTH		SECTOR ROTATION	
	Conservative	Aggressive	Growth and value	Conservative	Aggressive	Conservative	Aggressive
Large cap stocks	*Ivy Canadian *Optima Strategy Equity Section	*Templeton Heritage Retirement	*20/20 Canadian Growth * Ethical Growth		*Trimark RSP Equity *Trimark Select Canadian	*Industrial Horizon	*AGF Cdn. Equity *C.I. Cdn. Growth

	Conservative	Aggressive	Growth and value	Conservative	Aggressive	Conservative	Aggressive
	VALUE		**BLEND**	**GROWTH**		**SECTOR ROTATION**	
			* Fidelity Capital Builder		Growth		
Medium cap Growth stocks		* Global Strategy Canada Growth	* BT Landmark Canadian		* Industrial Future *Trimark Canadian	* AIC Advantage	* Dynamic Cdn. * Industrial Equity * Industrial Future * Industrial Growth * Industrial Pension * Mackenzie Equity
Small cap stocks Growth			*BT Landmark Small	* Cundill Security	* Working Ventures		* Altamira (all) *AGF Growth Equity *Dynamic Fund of Canada * Universal Cdn. Equity

Courtesy Equion Group

THE OTHER SECTOR FUNDS: DEFERRING CAPITAL GAINS FOR AS LONG AS YOU WANT

Sector funds are open-ended mutual funds with several different classes of special shares. Monies invested in each of these special shares are used to purchase units in the corresponding fund and act like a preferred share until the total disposition of your holdings. Only then do you realize capital gains. Moving your assets between different funds (i.e., emerging markets, Canadian, Pacific, money markets) depending on market, tax and interest rate conditions triggers no gains or taxes. These sector funds will benefit primarily those investors who need to shelter capital gains, and are in a high income tax bracket who seek to actively manage their own portfolios and need the flexibility and diversification to move in and out of equities without short-term tax consequences. Table 4.3 illustrates the benefit of a Sector Fund. The Sector Funds are currently available for 1994 under present legislation left unaffected by the budget. Canadian International is the largest supplier of this product to the market in Canada. They are available from your independent financial planner or broker. We believe Sector Funds will become increasingly popular with Canadians in 1994/1995. AGF also offers a similar product called AGF International.

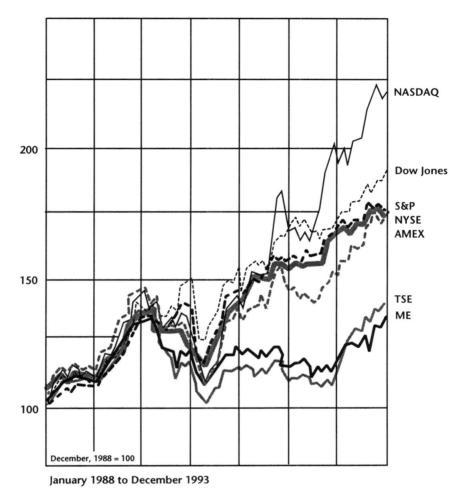

Figure 4.3: North American Indexes

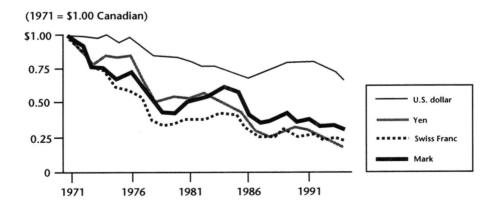

Figure 4.4: Decline in the Canadian Dollar

57

Table 4.3: Benefits of Deferring Taxes

The table below illustrates the benefits of deferring taxes. It assumes a 12 percent annual return, a 20-year holding period and annual rotation of investments.

	AFTER-TAX VALUE		
END OF YEAR	INTEREST INCOME (50% TAX)	CAPITAL GAINS (37.5% TAX)	SECTOR FUND OR AGF INT'L
0	100,000	100,000	100,000
1	106,000	107,500	112,000
2	112,360	115,563	125,440
3	119,102	124,230	140,493
4	126,248	133,547	157,352
5	133,823	143,563	176,234
6	141,852	154,330	197,382
7	150,363	165,905	221,068
8	159,385	178,348	247,596
9	168,948	191,724	277,308
10	179,085	206,103	310,585
11	189,830	221,561	347,855
12	201,220	238,178	389,598
13	213,293	256,041	436,349
14	226,090	275,244	488,711
15	239,656	295,888	547,347
16	254,035	318,079	613,039
17	269,277	341,935	686,604
18	285,434	367,580	768,997
19	302,560	395,149	861,276
20	320,714	424,785	964,629
Tax on disposition			$324,236
After tax-value			$640,393

HOW TO KNOW WHEN TO GET OUT OF YOUR MUTUAL FUND

Canadians are always hesitant to sell a fund (even a bad fund which consistently lags the market). It's even harder to sell a good one that has made you a lot of money. I regularly cite the reference to Altamira Equity Fund that was one of the best four-year performers between 1989 and 1992, yet missed the market in the last six months of 1993 and produced returns of 2.5 per cent versus 40 per cent in the first six months of the year, and negative numbers in early 1994.

Costs are one criterion for knowing when to get out of your fund. Tax implications and costs of redemptions are important. Watch annual expenses, and if they rise with the fund's success and growth, look to get out. Watch small funds that do well historically then performance begins to lag. Watch for market making and self-fulfilling prophecies. If they have a lot of money, they may buy shares in a small firm from two or three of their different funds, thereby producing a share price rise. It doesn't take a genius to make money doing this but it is a questionable long-term strategy. Be patient with a good fund. Long-term stars tend to remain long-term stars. If, however, a good fund has three bad years, it's time to get out. If there is new management, give the new manager at least 12 to 18 months to establish his style.

Magnetism of the Mean

All strategies regress towards the mean over time. Therefore, invest in the mean and save commissions and trades. We examined the performance of value growth and small company funds over the past 14 years in Canada. Over time they had peaks and valleys and continuously underperformed market averages.

Occam's Razor: 14th-Century Thesis

When there are multiple solutions to a problem, choose the simplest one.

Figure 4.5: Reasons to Cash Out Your Shares

- Performance is poor relative to similar mutual funds, or to companies in the same industry and sector.

- You lose faith in management either because the company or the fund is experimenting with a new strategy or you sense a lack of candor. The replacement of a mutual fund's portfolio manager is crucial to monitor.

- The stock price is no longer reasonable in relation to company fundamentals, such as earnings and dividends. Be wary of high debt as a percentage of capital. For mutual funds, make sure the manager abides by a stated "sell discipline" that takes these factors into account.

- External forces are unfavourable. The company's products may be becoming obsolete or its market could be shrinking. As in the case of cigarettes, government intervention is often a good time to clear out of a sector.

- Your emotions are getting in the way. Don't get so attached to a stock or a fund that you won't sell if it takes a dive or never performs to expectations. Also, if you are so worried about a company or a fund that you can't sleep at night, dump it.

- You need to diversify your holdings or adjust for your changing risk tolerance. But the best reason to sell is because you've achieved your goal.

WHAT THE EXPERTS SAY

John Templeton: The true founder of modern mutual funds and the Templeton Group of Funds.

1) 60 per cent of market value is outside North America.

2) If emerging markets go up too high, stay in safer developed country markets.

3) Japanese stocks are selling at 55 times earnings. This has no relation to income, dividends or earnings.

4) I see a 6,000 Dow Jones Average by the year 2000.

Peter Lynch: The guru who directed Fidelity Magellon up 2,800 per cent from 1977 to 1990.

1) If you don't need your money for several years, go to mutual funds and establish a portfolio.

2) Don't try to change your portfolio too frequently.

3) Have several different categories of funds to increase diversification and reduce risk.

Michael Evans: Editor of the *Portfolio Planner* newsletter and the top mutual fund handicapper of the decade.

1) I never recommend bond funds, except for a small window of opportunity when bond prices are rising as stocks are falling. Stocks will always outperform bonds.

2) Last year's winners are this year's losers.

3) Stay away from sector funds. If you are investing for the long run, common sense tells you that the portfolio manager with the flexibility to pick any stock instead of only gold or oil or one country will be able to select better stocks.

4) Avoid very small, very young funds with less than $50 million. Pick ones that outperformed the market by 10 per cent or more over the last three years.

Our Own Research

1) 90 per cent of mutual fund selection success comes from selecting the right category of funds, and only 10 per cent from selecting the right fund in a given year.

2) High expenses share a strong correlation with poor returns from bond funds.

3) Index funds outperform at least 70 per cent of all funds especially if held for a period of time.

4) Asset allocation funds are really market timers. They have been marketed as one-stop low-risk investments and only go up. They have not delivered. These funds are built on regular adjustments to portfolios. They are diversified as you should be. They are really fancy versions of balanced funds which keep fixed balances.

5) I like index funds for many reasons. They are cheap, with low expenses. It is difficult for the average Canadian investor to have the time to pay close attention to all their holdings and still beat market odds. There is little extra risk compared to the market in general. (We will explain Beta values in #8 below. Index funds are usually 1.00 Beta's.) Index funds take losses in serious bear markets, but only average losses — not deep ones. They are also superior because they are fully invested in the market at all times. Most equity or balanced funds have cash balances and frequent trades and transaction costs that reduce returns by adding to costs.

6) Sector Funds for speculation. Sector Funds are bought for specific purposes and should not be part of the portfolio. Their pattern is built on the fact that people buy them near the peak and sell near the trough. They are largely only for speculators. They have high sales charges and high expense-ratio transaction costs engendered both by surging cash inflows and outflows and 200 per cent per annum portfolio turnover.

7) Correlated versus Differentiated Funds. The key determinant of performance of an equity mutual fund is the performance of the stock market as a whole as measured by the TSE 300 or Standard & Poors 500 in the U.S.

The market's performance explains 85 per cent of the total return of most growth, value and equity income funds. These are called Correlated Funds. Those that do not follow this pattern — small cap funds, specialty or sector funds, international funds and gold/precious metal funds — are called Differentiated Funds.

The market S&P 500 explains:
- 85 per cent of the return of growth, value and equity income funds
- 70 per cent of the return of small cap funds
- 60 per cent of the return of sector or specialty funds
- 40 per cent of the returns of international funds
- 0 per cent of the return of precious metal and gold funds

8) These are the most reliable analytical criteria to use.
- R^2 — the relationship between a fund's return and a market index such as the S&P 500 or TSE 300.

R^2 normally runs at 80 per cent to 90 per cent, meaning a high proportion of its total return is explained by the performance of the overall stock market. The remaining 20 per cent or less is explained by 1) the fund's basic strategy; and 2) the tactics and investment selections of the fund's portfolio manager.

An R^2 below 80 per cent means significantly less predictability of relative performance.

An R^2 of 95 per cent means the funds return has been shaped predominantly by the action of the market itself.

An index return would have R^2 of 100 per cent.

• Beta is a measure of risk. It includes a fund's past price volatility relative to a particular stock index. Most high-correlation funds have Betas of .85 to 1.05, close to the 1.00 represented by the market in aggregate.

Very conservative stock funds will register a Beta of .75, meaning that in a 10 per cent market decline the stock fund's value is expected to fall only 7.5 per cent. An aggressive stock fund will have a Beta of 1.25, which means that their values will fall 12.5 per cent if the market falls 10 per cent. The same applies if the market rises. Beta is a rough proxy of your price volatility expectations.

To properly analyze a fund for low risk and conservative volatility, we look at expenses, income (gross yield), R^2 and Beta. This will give accurate measures of risk and return, what percent of its performance is explained by general market conditions, its total degree of risk, and what return we are getting for the risk of the fund.

9) No Load — Not Really. No-load mutual funds are ideal for investors who know what they are buying and need no financial advice or planning. Many have done very well for Canadians. A no-load fund has no front-end sales commission when you buy it and usually no back-end fee if you sell it in the short term, so the cost of buying and selling it is less.

You are buying the fund directly from the mutual company. However, there are usually the following charges attached:

• If you buy it through a broker or discount dealer there is normally a commission charge of, say, $50 on a $10,000 purchase.

• There is normally a $40 or more charge to open up an account with the mutual fund company.

• You may pay a fee of up to 2 per cent of the net asset value of your holdings when you transfer from one fund to another within the same collection of funds from the same company. Many have imposed annual limitations on the number of transfers you may make in a given year.

• Many banks and trust companies impose close-out fees if you redeem all of your money from a fund.

• If you put the mutual fund in an RRSP, they will charge an annual trustee fee of $175 to $200. Make sure you pay this fee outside your account to make it tax deductible. If it is deducted from your account, it is not.

• If you need to withdraw money on a regular basis from a no-load plan, there will be systematic withdrawal fees as well.

Remember!! Nothing is for nothing and you get what you pay for.

10) Watch for the Concealed Dangers. Many funds are actively involved in the futures and derivatives market just as the big hedge players like George Soros was when he lost U.S.$600 million.

Derivatives mean performance is derived from something else in an attempt to reduce risk, protect the fund from market slides or to enhance returns. These funds were bought by many who were moving out of GICs and bonds and have degrees of risk they have never understood. But since investing is about risk the derivatives failed and risk actually rose. Read the prospectus carefully and attend the frequent information meetings offered by these companies. Ask about derivative and hedge exposure.

11) If you pay a load on the fund, it is usually best to select either a fair front-end load or a deferred load that declines the longer you hold the fund. After three years, there is little statistical performance difference between front end and no-load funds, especially for equity investors.

12) Avoid a level load or annual flat charge at all costs.

The above issues were presented to help you separate the facts from the fiction and the mythology and hype from the researched realities.

Conclusions for the Conservative Investor

My interviews with over a dozen fund manages in Canada, the U.S. and Hong Kong and over 200 financial planners and brokers led me to the following conclusions for the Conservative Investor:

1) For the long haul, you are better off in an index fund. They mimic market performance at a low cost. Only about 10 per cent of fund managers can add real above average value over time.

2) Don't just invest on the record. It's one criterion. A person who is a consistent five- or 10-year winner has a higher probability of winning more often then losing, but no one is perfect. Even Peter Lynch in *One Up on Wall Street* admitted that in his last seven years, he only beat the market by 3 per cent on average — and he was the "boy wonder."

3) Avoid the stinkers. The really bad funds rarely get any better. Avoid bottom dwellers. They are not undervalued bargains. They will have high expenses and changing management.

4) The best deals come from the big companies. They have the resources to hire the best people, the best technology and demand competence on the job.

5) The longest-term managers have the most consistent results. Poor performers usually get the chop, anyway.

6) Look at short-term performance fluctuation as a measure of risk. If you want low risk, make sure the fund stays that way. Over time, avoid volatility.

7) If the fund is a stellar bull market performer, expect it to drop like a stone in the bear market and with more risk, and vice versa. Conservative Investors want consistency in both market conditions.

8) All funds have costs — even "no loads." If you need advice, expect to pay for it. If not, don't.

9) Make sure the fund has a focus: capital gains, income or dividends, but not all of the above. Focused funds do better as they have a single-minded goal and are more efficient.

10) The 25 per cent of funds with the lowest costs had the best returns. With bonds, the bigger the fund, the lower the costs.

11) Balanced funds are more ideal as part of the debt component of your portfolio. They seem to do moderately well in all conditions. Global balanced funds with triple A bonds and equities from major global markets seem to be appropriate in many adverse situations.

Here are some questions the Conservative Investor should ask before they buy.

1) Is the fund too risky for my needs and taste?

2) Are the fund's stated investment objectives in line with mine?

3) Is the fund similar to something I already own and therefore not really a diversification?

4) How does the fund's performance compare to funds with similar styles?

5) Is the manager who did the best work still involved with the fund?

6) Has the fund grown so big that its past performance cannot be duplicated?

7) Are the fund's fees and expenses reasonable?

8) Was the fund invested in a single stock or sector for a while, or in cash when rates were high in order to get its good results?

9) Has the fund been a consistent performer?

10) Where did the fund's income come from? If you are an older Conservative Investor, you'll want regular income distribution. Then income is important.

FINALLY

For a fee, a thousand different experts will gladly try to tell you which stocks will go up and down, but is their advice any better than just chance?

Economists, who have little belief in expert opinion, are generally of the view that we should be skeptical of any system that works better than chance. Yet some mutual fund "experts" have outperformed the market in the last 10 years.

Research shows that, over the past 10 years, fund managers who concentrate on growth and capital appreciation beat the market. Research also shows that, in the short term, funds with exceptional returns in one year outperformed the average in the next year 65 per cent of the time.

Success seems to be measured in going backward, not forward. Unsuccessful funds are allowed to die and are excluded from the comparative numbers. Therefore, numbers are "survivor biased." When times are good, big mutual fund companies start large numbers of funds. When this factor is included in the statistical analysis, the numbers dwindle and this "hot hand" feature seems to come and go.

Results show that if you invested in the Top 20 funds of the 1980s for the 1990s, you would have dramatically underperformed the market.

Therefore, is there really a science to the selection of funds? One that will reduce your risk and enhance your long-term return? The answer is perhaps. Here are some of the keys that appear to work more often than not.

1) Diversification: Never buy one fund, but buy a portfolio in each category. Three to five equity funds, two or three bond funds and one or two money market funds. This reduces risk.

2) Invest outside of North America to be sure you participate in economic success somewhere.

3) Follow the interest rate cycle. If rates go over 9 per cent, you need more money market holdings and less equity. If they fall below 9 per cent, you need more equities.

4) Buy mutual funds with the lowest operating costs. There is a negative relationship between expenses and the rates of return.

5) If you are really risk averse, remember that funds tied to market indexes tend to be the ones that outperform the competition over time. They are never big winners — just consistent gainers. There are Canadian and U.S. index funds.

6) If you like a lot of risk, the best choices are the hedge funds that are tied to market puts, calls, options and futures. They seem to be able to hire the best talent and produce the biggest gains or losses. There are only a few Canadian funds to choose from in this category.

CHAPTER FIVE

International Investment Strategy

I nternational diversification has not as yet produced all of the returns that were hoped for. Japan disappointed, followed by Hong Kong and Mexico. The U.S. has been one of the poorest performers for the past dozen years. Yet we cannot deny the global linkages in markets.

The correlation between Hong Kong and New York Stock Exchanges is .48, which means that 48 per cent of the movement in Hong Kong is a result of general trends in the New York Stock Exchange, and markets are moving closer together.

The Toronto market is only 2.6 per cent of global stock markets' capitalization. Canada represents less than 4 per cent of world trade. International relationships are simply the reality of the 1990s. Therefore, Canadians need foreign content in our portfolios. We need to understand the risk of these markets, which ways to participate in them and how to select international investments that will not endanger capital.

The danger is to be caught up in the trends and the vogue of the markets. In 1990, it was Japan. In 1992-93, it was Hong Kong and smaller Asian markets, and then emerging markets in South America. The pitfall is that most people invest in these markets when they are at their peak or are caught in the move from fixed-income securities to these high-risk, volatile and, at times, dangerous options.

Emerging market investments in South and Central America, emerging Asian markets and Eastern Europe are not developed enough, diversified enough or stable enough in political/economic terms to be of present relevance to the Conservative Investor.

On the other hand, most of Western Europe and the major U.S. equities are secure and stable markets with clear controls and regulation and a strong short- to medium-term potential.

We need not just consider equities. Mutual funds, balanced funds, and European currency fixed-income securities are all viable international investment components.

MARKET DANGERS

Hong Kong is a place I find thrilling regardless of 1997 and the Chinese takeover. Hong Kong is 30 per cent of the GDP of China and is now among the Top 10 exporters in the world.

Real estate is more valuable than gold here and is highly overvalued. Economists call this region the economy of 21st Century and North American yesterdays.

Hong Kong is the most stable and most representative of Asian markets, except Japan. It represents 496 stocks on the Hung Seng exchange producing 3 per cent yields at a price/earnings multiple of 16 for the total market. One hundred dollars I invested in the Hong Kong Index in April 1986 is worth over $500 today. The members of the exchange are growing in size with greater mainland China exposure. This is the disturbing part. I do not believe China's revolution in free markets will continue at 10 per cent to 12 per cent per annum growth, and potential violence from the interior agricultural provinces is a threat as is the corruption I have seen from firsthand visits.

Only after 1997 will this market have clarity and a more solid focus. It will be more volatile than Korea.

Philippines and Thailand are great low-cost producers with burgeoning economies. Singapore is spectacular and organized with superb real estate and the best-quality canes in Asia.

Table 5.1: Major Markets: How They're Valued

COUNTRY	P/E RATIO
Canada	78.9
Japan	77.8
Austria	73.4
Norway	41.9
Malaysia	35.5
Germany	30.6
France	29.5
Singapore	24.6
New Zealand	21.8
United States	20.5
Switzerland	20.3
United Kingdom	20.0

Spain	19.9
Hong Kong	19.3

The lower the price-to-earnings (P/E) ratio, the cheaper a stock is. A stock can rise in price, but if its earnings rise even more, then the stock price still has more room to rise. This same measure can be applied to the entire stock market of a country. Indeed, it can be applied to all the world's stock exchanges. Morgan Stanley reckons the world index as having a P/E ratio of 28.7 — on the high side. But some individual markets are quite a bit higher and some are lower. (All measures are as of 28/2/94.)

Table 5.2: Top 10 World Equity Markets: Annualized Total Returns 1982–1992

RANK	MARKET	% RETURN*
1.	Hong Kong	25.5
2.	Belgium	25.4
3.	France	23.1
4.	The Netherlands	22.1
5.	Spain	20.9
6.	Austria	20.3
7.	United Kingdom	19.9
8.	Sweden	17.6
9.	Switzerland	17.0
10.	Norway	16.5

* In U.S. Dollars

Figure 5.1: World View — 41 Markets at a Glance

COUNTRY	1993 TOTAL RETURN	1993 PRICE-TO EARNINGS RATIO	5-YEAR P/E RATIO AVERAGE	1993 PRICE-TO- BOOK VALUE	5-YEAR PAY RATIO AVERAGE	9-YEAR COMPOUND RATE OF RETURN	BIGGEST DECLINE (YEAR) (SINCE 1984)
ARGENTINA	72.30%	41.48	64.08	1.96	1.25	40.69%	–36.5% ('90)
AUSTRALIA	33.37%	18.92	15.60	1.95	1.46	14.06%	–17.0% ('90)
AUSTRIA	31.98%	34.53	37.40	1.87	2.11	13.09%	–13.9% ('92)
BELGIUM	22.08%	16.77	12.90	1.51	1.53	17.48%	–10.3% ('90)
BRAZIL	99.40%	12.59	2.84	0.55	0.55	13.67%	–65.7% ('90)
CANADA	17.42%	25.75	33.30	1.74	1.48	7.24%	–12.3% ('92)
CHILE	34.60%	20.04	12.48	2.11	1.50	52.51%	–23.7% ('84)
COLOMBIA	34.70%	25.54	21.47	1.80	1.48	45.51%	–12.3% ('88)

69

COUNTRY	1993 TOTAL RETURN	1993 PRICE-TO EARNINGS RATIO	5-YEAR P/E RATIO AVERAGE	1993 PRICE-TO BOOK VALUE	5-YEAR PAY RATIO AVERAGE	9-YEAR COMPOUND DATE OF RETURN	BIGGEST DECLINE (YEAR) (SINCE 1984)
DENMARK	32.80%	31.32	10.90	2.28	1.86	12.77%	−29.1% ('92)
FINLAND*	76.97%	24.04	13.60	1.27	0.89	2.16%	−22.0% ('91)
FRANCE	19.56%	23.08	14.30	1.70	1.69	16.27%	−12.8% ('90)
GERMANY	34.79%	24.79	16.60	2.22	1.96	9.43%	−21.0% ('87)
GREECE	21.90%	10.18	12.21	1.94	2.48	22.62%	−37.6% ('88)
HONG KONG	120.85%	21.18	12.70	2.78	1.61	28.65%	−7.8% ('87)
INDIA	18.60%	39.70	26.31	4.90	3.80	19.40%	−15.6%('87)%
INDONESIA**	113.40%	28.93	25.93	3.09	3.11	5.91%	−42.3% ('91)
IRELAND	36.41%	16.63	N/A	2.13	N/A	16.48%	−15.6% ('92)
ITALY	25.00%	21.08	48.20	0.59	1.35	6.97%	−24.5% ('92)
JAPAN	23.90%	50.13	43.60	2.02	2.95	11.53%	−36.4% ('90)
JORDAN	24.20%	17.95	12.91	1.96	1.60	9.48%	−12.2% ('84)
MALAYSIA	126.24%	43.49	27.54	5.39	3.06	27.09%	−14.2% ('85)
MEXICO	44.89%	16.50	12.90	3.18	1.66	54.07%	− 4.8% ('87)
NETHERLANDS	31.51%	17.14	12.90	2.02	1.43	15.72%	−2.3% ('90)
NEW ZEALAND	58.33%	23.64	18.00	1.83	1.16	9.05%	−35.4% ('90)
NORWAY	30.45%	18.09	32.50	2.10	2.29	7.89%	−21.5% ('92)
PAKISTAN	56.20%	27.64	17.67	4.20	2.50	24.53%	−18.4% ('92)
PHILIPPINES	133.86%	38.69	17.90	5.23	3.28	53.71%	−53.9% ('90)
PORTUGAL*	36.50%	17.76	13.73	1.68	1.82	14.40%	−29.8% ('90)
SINGAPORE	72.26%	20.22	19.30	2.46	1.88	24.71%	−8.1% ('90)
SOUTH AFRICA	80.39%	19.20	N/A	2.66	N/A	17.94%	−38.7% ('92)
SOUTH KOREA	20.90%	25.12	22.49	1.38	1.39	22.62%	−25.4% ('90)
SPAIN	19.50%	15.85	12.00	1.39	1.17	17.61%	−21.2% ('92)
SWEDEN	18.62%	22.34	7.90	2.36	1.99	15.36%	−15.0% ('90)
SWITZERLAND	41.71%	16.79	15.70	1.81	1.62	11.50%	−14.9% ('87)
TAIWAN	69.00%	34.73	30.42	3.93	4.82	26.88%	−50.9% ('90)
THAILAND	103.00%	27.54	15.71	4.71	2.90	38.11%	−20.7% ('90)
TURKEY*	234.30%	36.34	17.35	7.18	4.30	33.59%	−61.1% ('88)
U.K.	18.96%	18.69	14.70	2.36	1.90	15.34%	−2.3% ('92)
U.S.***	11.28%	23.10	19.76	3.72	3.56	14.20%	−6.2% ('90)
VENEZUELA	-6.90%	17.44	18.34	1.85	2.25	18.97%	−42.3% ('92)
ZIMBABWE	143.60%	8.83	6.11	0.91	0.93	28.23%	−59.8% ('92)

* 7-year cumulative rate of return ** 4-year cumulative rate of return ***Wilshire 5000 Equity Index, 10-year compounded return. Source: International Finance Corp.'s Global Index, Ft Actuaries Index, Goldman Sachs & Co., Morgan Stanley Capital International

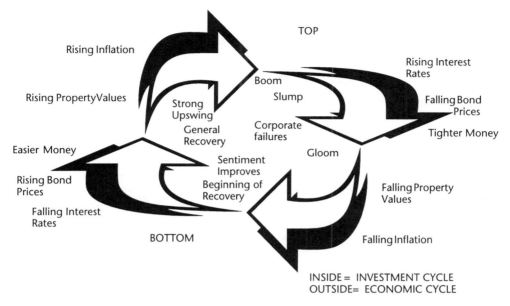

Figure 5.2: The Relationship between Economics and Investing

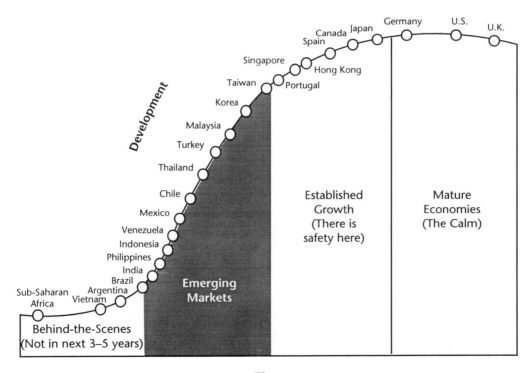

Figure 5.3: The Market Cycle

71

Vietnam will come onstream in 1995-1996. The French and Germans have been buying everything in sight here for development and now, as the U.S. is moving in, Vietnam will become the Paris of the Orient. The stock market will be a Wild West show and as risky as Poland or Turkey for at least a decade.

India was on my speculative pick list for 1994 and Bombay has become a mega winner with 2,000 companies and explosive growth in the Indian middle class, but it is still a high-risk market. All these are markets for the young and risk-oriented speculator. A good 5 per cent component of the equity mix of the speculative investor offers big wins or big reversals year to year.

South and Central America have similarities to Asia with some mature and many emerging markets. Chile is the market leader, Argentina the country in mature transition. Brazil is in transformation, Peru and Venezuela are potentially exciting, and Costa Rica is the Riviera and Switzerland of the region.

Mexico is part of North America and a continuous disappointment. It should be doing better, but except for the northern regions on the U.S. border and Mexico City, it has failed despite the enormous impact of the North American Free Trade Agreement.

Political stability is essential for Mexico to offer investment potential. Once again, these markets have been exciting but dangerous except for the risk oriented. It will take another three to five years for there to be real clarity and direction here.

China is a mystery and a great attraction. Shanghai offers 155 state-controlled enterprises with "A" shares for mainland Chinese investors and 28 with "B" shares for foreigners denominated in dollars. Most "B" shares are in state-owned companies that are overvalued in inefficient and bankrupt firms. Accounting is questionable and multiples make little sense whatsoever.

It will take at least two years of price stability and political and civil order for this market to make sense for international investors. Therefore, it must be treated as highly speculative.

Japan is an enigma, a market in an established near-mature economy that can rise to 36,000 on the NIKKEI and fall to 15,000 in six months and then rise to 21,000 in four months. The swings seem unreasonable and frightening.

The economy experienced its worst recession since the 1950s and then recovered because of loosening credit, but the politics are still a mess. The population is old and ageing, and unemployment is becoming more prevalent.

Japan should be in everyone's portfolio in some way for the long term, but the problems are often hidden and the financial sector may be its own worst enemy. Banks have heavily invested in major industrials which overinvested in real estate from Tokyo to New York and took massive losses. Small investors got massacred in the market collapse and many lost their life savings. Things should be regulated and the industry less collusive and rapacious.

This is a closed society of hard workers who consistently surprise us. No one picked the recovery in Japan to be as quick, yet it is not deep and one-day scandals can cause a 3 per cent to 5 per cent loss. This is not for the faint-hearted.

	GDP		CONSUMER PRICES	
	1993	1994	1993	1994
Czech Republic	-1.00%	2.00%	21.00%	11.00%
Hungary	-2.00%	1.00%	23.00%	23.00%
Poland	4.00%	4.00%	35.00%	30.00%
Slovakia	-4.00%	-2.00%	23.00%	20.00%
Bulgaria	-5.00%	-2.00%	73.00%	55.00%
Romania	1.00%	2.00%	256.00%	200.00%
Russia	-12.00%	-7.00%	930.00%	500.00%
Ukraine	-15.00%	-23.00%	3700.00%	1000.00%

ECONOMIC GROWTH PROSPECTS

	1965 TO 1989 %	1993 TO 2000 FORECAST %
East Asia	7.2	6.7
South Asia	4.2	4.7
Europe, North Africa & Middle East	4.2	3.6
Latin America & Caribbean	4.3	5.0
Emerging Markets Universe	5.1	6.5
All Developing Countries	4.7	5.2
Industrial Countries	3.1	2.5

Figure 5.4: Direct Foreign Investment, 1989 through 1993, and Economic Growth Prospects

We may be gambling a bit here, but even the most conservative of Canadians needs a tiny bit of speculation. Once again, never more than 5 per cent of the equity side of your portfolio and only in a broad-based Japanese blue chip equity fund, but it may be worth the risk if you're under 65 and can hold for three to five years.

The former Eastern European bloc is doing much better in many areas. The Polish market is tiny and embryonic, very much a place for promoters. It can rise and fall 30 per cent to 50 per cent per annum. Hungary and both the Czech and Slovak Republics will be good for investment in three to five years. Forget about everything and everywhere else in the East.

Asia, Turkey and Israel have drawn great attention as has South Africa for 1995. Israel and Turkey were spectacular in 1993 and fell sharply in 1994. Political stability and real peace will make Israel the Hong Kong of the Mediterranean, and South Africa the New York of Africa, but not today.

A BIAS TO STABILITY

Our investment strategy must be biased towards established markets in the next one to three years as these new markets age and gain maturity.

The choices are limited to major Western European markets and the U.S. The currencies are the most stable. The Canadian dollar has lost 19 per cent of its value against the U.S. dollar since 1991.

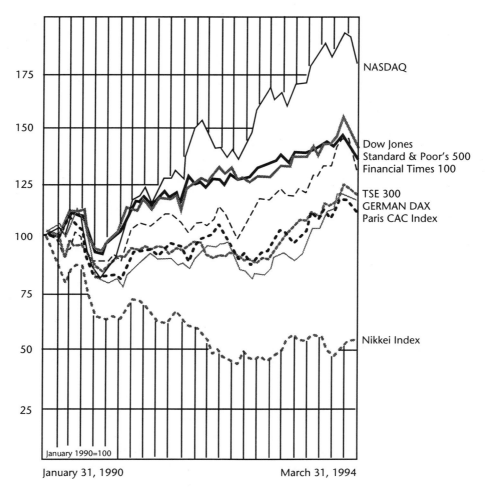

Figure 5.5: International Stock Exchanges

Well-known Canadian financier Andrew Sarlos forecasted in a speech in Montreal in January 1994 that the political and debt crisis could drive the dollar as low as U.S. 65¢. We need to protect ourselves in the following ways:

1) International Bond Funds either for RRSPs or portfolios only if interest rates are declining in Europe.

74

2) International Equity Funds if they are heavily invested in Western Europe, at least 75 per cent.

3) International or Global Balanced Funds with 30 per cent or less in bonds and heavy European and major U.S. content.

4) U.S. Pay Stocks especially for RRSPs, Canadian shares of Canadian blue chips in U.S. dollars and dividends in U.S. dollars.

5) Canadian Foreign Currency Bonds (RRSP) Corporate and Canadian Government Bonds have been issued in foreign currencies as 40 per cent of our debt is borrowed offshore. We can buy them in Swiss Francs, German Marks, Japanese Yen or U.S. dollars, yet they qualify as Canadian investments as they are issued in Canada.

Table 5.3: World Markets January 1, 1994 to May 15, 1994

COUNTRY	PERFORMANCE IN U.S. DOLLARS				IN LOCAL CURRENCY			
	INDEX	YTD S% CHG.	YTD RANK	DIVIDEND YIELD	INDEX	YTD % CHG.	EXCHANGE RATE TO $	YTD % CHG.
Australia	175.22	5	8	3.42	160.05	-2.1	1.3734	7.3
Austria	180.04	-2.7	17	1.06	153.94	-7.6	11.5795	5.3
Belgium	176.56	8.6	6	3.73	147.53	1.7	33.8825	6.7
Britain	193.31	-5.7	21	3.92	189.82	-7.6	0.6623	2.1
Canada	131.42	-3.2	19	2.57	131	0.6	1.3766	-3.8
Denmark	256.53	3.8	9	1.31	224.53	-1.7	6.4355	5.6
Finland	155.98	26.6	2	0.83	176.96	17.5	5.3752	7.7
France	177.11	0.7	14	2.88	156.4	-4	5.6295	4.9
Germany	145.17	3.5	10	1.66	124.25	-1.9	1.6463	5.5
Hong Kong	394.61	-19.4	24	2.72	391.37	-19.4	7.7251	0
Ireland	189.69	2.4	11	3.38	179.45	-3.1	0.6714	5.7
Italy	93.18	35.9	1	1.41	109.95	25.4	1580	8.4
Japan	158.55	21.8	3	0.77	104.14	13.4	103.91	7.4
Malaysia	478.15	-19.2	23	1.4	476.33	-22.3	2.5893	4
Mexico	2058.5	-13.8	22	1.04	7465.33	-7.9	3.317	-6.4
Netherlands	203.91	2.4	12	3.27	171.87	-2.6	1.8467	5.2
New Zealand	69.3	2	13	3.81	62.7	-2.7	1.7039	4.9
Norway	202.68	12.8	5	1.69	196.1	6.9	7.1282	5.5
Singapore	352.77	-4	20	1.52	250.08	-8.2	1.5383	4.6
South Africa	259.1	-3	18	2.22	278.91	11.3	4.925	-12.9
Spain	149.99	7.6	7	3.86	154.56	2.4	136.025	5.1

PERFORMANCE IN U.S. DOLLARS					IN LOCAL CURRENCY			
COUNTRY	INDEX	YTD S% CHG.	YTD RANK	DIVIDEND YIELD	INDEX	YTD % CHG.	EXCHANGE RATE TO $	YTD % CHG.
Sweden	229.72	17	4	1.53	260.76	7.6	7.6678	8.7
Switzerland	159.63	-0.3	15	1.75	139.05	-5.7	1.4051	5.7
United States	185.43	-0.4	16	2.88	185.43	-2.4		
COMPOSITE INDEXES								
Europe	171.94	0.8	1.4	2.89	160.33	-2.9		
Europe/Pacific	169.21	1.1	9.1	1.83	132.58	3.2		
World	174.22	1.6	4.2	2.21	151.47	1.1		

Source: Goldman, Sachs & Co. Exchange rates as of Friday's London Close.
© 1994 The Financial Times Ltd., and Natwest Securities Ltd.

This is only a snapshot and not a predictor of trends. Check out the Top 10.

6) International Agency Bonds (all still RRSP eligible), bonds issued by the World Bank, Asian Development Bank or Intern-American Development all qualify for RRSPs and are in foreign currencies and triple A-rated.

7) Offshore Investment Trusts for high-net-worth individuals set up in tax havens to protect yourself from Canadian taxes and potential capital gains on death.

8) Quality blue chip stocks from offshore:

Canon	Japan
Bayer	Germany
Rolls Royce	U.K.
Peugeot	France
Mitsubishi	Japan
Holderbank	Switzerland
Alitalia	Italy
Svedola	Sweden
Volvo	Sweden
TDK	Japan
Jardine Matheson	Hong Kong
Perigrine Investments	Hong Kong

9) Maximize foreign content of your self-directed RRSP using the above components. Dividends from Canadian equities lose their tax credit in the RRSP. The 1994 content level and that for years to come is limited to 20 per cent foreign content. Also select Canadian equity growth funds that have up to 20 per

cent foreign content in Western Europe and the U.S. This still counts as 100 per cent Canadian taking your legal foreign content, if you maximize in the category to 36 per cent. This will add up to 5 per cent incremental growth value per annum, tax free to the value of the RRSP.

10) Offshore cash: This is especially relevant for those who travel on holiday to the south, Caribbean, Hawaii, Mexico or Europe. You can establish a bank account in border cities with the U.S. or in the country you visit most often with a major international bank. This will give you liquidity, flexibility and lower cost. Personally, I never exchange currency in a major bank or trust company or buy traveller's cheques there either. Many currency exchanges such as Friedbergs, Thomas Cook and Forex among others will give you much better market rates on all major currencies, and most offer free traveller's cheques as well.

Table 5.4: The Best in Bonds

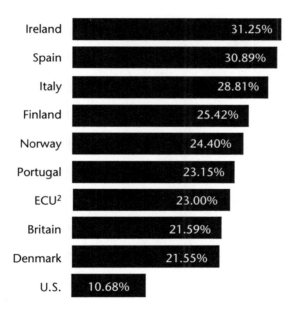

TOP-PERFORMING WORLD BOND MARKETS[1]

Ireland	31.25%
Spain	30.89%
Italy	28.81%
Finland	25.42%
Norway	24.40%
Portugal	23.15%
ECU[2]	23.00%
Britain	21.59%
Denmark	21.55%
U.S.	10.68%

[1]Total returns for 1993 (price change and interest income)
[2]European Currency Unit

CHAPTER SIX

Real Estate

Major tax changes on capital gains, the massive overbuilding of the market, the sharp drop in interest rates followed by a dramatic rise, and the changing demographics have altered the face of Canadian real estate for decades to come.

The next demographic cycle will start in 1997 and peak in 2005 when there will once again by a strong market demand and supply and demand equilibrium. We are now again buying accommodation and not investing. I have dealt with the real estate cycle and global trends in *Strategic Personal Investing: Gold Edition*.

For the Conservative Investor there will be many important issues affecting domestic real estate including:

1) Mortgages

2) How much you can afford

3) Reverse mortgages vs. systematic withdrawals

4) Is it logical to own a home today?

5) The tax benefits of the home

6) Real estate investment trusts

Most offshore real estate is not necessarily a viable option for the Conservative Investor. The only markets in North America that I have found that offer returns are for the retirement-oriented such as Orlando, Jacksonville, Naples, The Florida Keys, Scottsdale, Dallas and similar dynamic growth investment sectors.

Multi-unit residential buildings in limited partnerships domiciled in the above markets have produced returns of 6 per cent to 12 per cent per annum with 100 per cent occupancy and full financing for high-net-worth individuals.

Growth real estate in Canada is limited to secondary markets such as Kelowna, Victoria, Kingston and London, as well as low-cost affordable housing under $200,000 for young families. Few major markets show any upside potential except as presented by the real estate cycle.

MORTGAGE ISSUES

The single most important factor in reducing your real estate risk is the cost of your mortgage. In today's brave new real estate world, there are currently at least 14 different rates and terms ranging from six months to 10 years, that can be paid off weekly or monthly, and are open or closed. There is even a 25-year mortgage. And remember, the posted mortgage rate is never the actual rate. You are now expected to haggle. We found that if the posted variable rate was 7.5 per cent, you could get one for as low as 6.95 per cent with a cap at six months if rates were to rise.

The essence is to view the spread between the short- and long-term rates. For example if the long-term fixed rates are 9.5 per cent and the short-term variable rates are 6.75 per cent, you are clearly better off staying variable.

Banks report that up to 75 per cent of all renewals in 1994 to date are following my advice and renewing for 12 months or less. This is despite the strong urging for peace of mind by locking in for the long term. Anyone who did this under current circumstances and a spread of over 200 basis points short to long term probably has only a "piece of mind."

However, the first-time home buyer, having fixed their total carrying costs, should consider fixing rates for up to three years if rates stabilize and edge downward to ensure there is less risk if their salary is frozen.

All mortgages should be negotiable with a three-month penalty. But be careful; the lenders are trying to sneak in a clause called the "redating" in the fine print to prevent you from being able to prepay and go elsewhere. It is imperative to strike out the clause or go elsewhere.

Things to consider when you are renewing:

1) The cost of the money — the rate is everything.

2) If your cash flow is strong and job secure, reduce the amortization schedule from the traditional 25 years to 15 years and pay off more principal, especially if rates are lower.

3) The rule of thumb is $3 interest saved for every dollar of principal paid off.

4) At the time of renewal, make a lump payment to reduce the total. This can usually be done without penalty.

5) This is the time to consider transferring to another lender if you have been poorly serviced.

6) Many big institutions are fighting for business. They will waive legal, registration and appraisal fees. Ask for it.

7) Ask for two or three alternative bids on the rate. Remember that trust companies, insurance companies and banks and credit unions all want you.

8) Learn to negotiate, especially if you can bring the institutions your RRSP, credit cards and personal business. Everything is negotiable.

How Much Can You Afford?

One way not to get into trouble is not to over-extend yourself in your personal residence. The myth of 1980s was to buy the most expensive home you could afford. Then inflation and rising property values would produce massive tax-free capital gains when you sold. Unfortunately, this proved to be wrong and the banking community has been stuck with tens of thousands of powers of sale as real estate collapsed across Canada.

It is imperative to determine what you can afford and to stay within these limits. Don't let the agent drag you around to see things beyond your means — it's a standard ploy.

The following chart is designed for those who are reselling and buying another home. This is the instance where the biggest risk is incurred (not in the first-time buy).

First, figure out how big a mortgage cheque you can afford to write each month.

1) Gross monthly income $_____

2) Monthly instalment payments (car loans, credit cards, etc.) $_____

3) Monthly real estate tax and homeowner's insurance $_____

4) Multiply line 1 by 0.28 $_____

5) Enter line 3 $_____

6) Subtract line 5 from line 4 $_____

7) Multiply line 1 by 0.36 $_____

8) Add lines 2 and 3 $_____

9) Subtract line 8 from line 7 $_____

Now compare lines 6 and 9. The lesser amount is the approximate monthly mortgage payment for which you can qualify.

1) Estimated equity in your home (today's value minus your mortgage balance). Be conservative. $_____

2) Subtract closing costs and legal and land transfer taxes $_____

3) Subtract repairs and improvements needed before selling $_____

81

4) Subtract broker's commission (this ranges from 5 per cent to 8 per cent of the sale price of your home, depending on what's customary in your area and what you negotiate with your agent) $_____

5) Add savings you're prepared to spend on a downpayment $_____

6) TOTAL $_____

7) Maximum amount you can borrow. $_____

8) Divide line 7 by 0.75. This assumes at least 25 per cent down. $_____

9) Subtract line 7 from line 8 $_____

Line 8 tells you how much house you can afford right now — with one caveat. Line 9 is the amount of cash you must put down to get the loan amount in line 7. If you don't have that much money for a downpayment (see line 6), you'll have to find a lender that will let you get away with a smaller downpayment. Either that or you'll have to lower your sights and buy a cheaper home. How much cheaper? Divide line 6 by 0.20. That's your top-dollar price.

Say No to Reverse Mortgages

For older retired Canadians who have little liquidity because they have over-invested in their home and did not properly plan for their future, the great salvation was to be the highly touted "reverse annuity mortgage" or, as some credit unions now offer, the reverse mortgage line of credit.

I say touted because several major national newspapers carried stories as to how great this would be for the elderly and what a deal it was. Unfortunately, these writers do not understand the issues.

The University of British Columbia study of older Canadians' financial situation showed us that 94 per cent of home owners over 75 have no mortgage, and 55 per cent of households are owned by people over the age of 75.

If reverse mortgages are a legitimate viable product, and a good deal that was fair and equitable to both parties, why is it that no major bank, trust or insurance company considers this a viable market or offers reverse annuity mortgages? Reverse mortgages are not regulated by any level of government, and as the average client is 70 and probably financially unsophisticated, they are sold on the concept. It is not something I would recommend to the Conservative Investor under any circumstances.

The only market for the reverse mortgage is someone over 75 with no desire to leave an estate. You are better off if you:

1) Sell your home — buy a less expensive one and invest the difference.

2) Rent out part of your home for cash flow.

3) Establish a home business.

4) Sell your home and rent, investing the total principal and living for free on the income stream with the capital intact.

5) Establish a total portfolio systematic withdrawal plan. If you structure it properly, as I suggest, you can draw down on average of 9.5 per cent per annum yet leave all capital intact. If you draw at 11.5 per cent, your capital will be secure for 30 years assuming average performance.

A good financial planner or broker can set this up for you. It will reduce your taxes but keep assets intact. The benefit is so superior that systematic withdrawal has been established on a broad basis for mutual fund programs as well.

IS IT LOGICAL TO OWN A HOME?

With the softening of the real estate market in the late 1980s, many people began to realize that the decision to purchase a home was more of a "quality of life" issue and less of an "investment" issue.

However, in 1994, with the changes in the federal budget and the ever-increasing burden of federal and provincial taxation, things have changed yet again. With real estate values finally levelling out, there is a clear advantage now for considering the purchase of a home.

The federal government ended the capital gains exemption on investment real estate in its February 1992 budget, and in its budget this past February, it ended the $100,000 capital gains exception altogether. The only remaining opportunity for sheltering capital gains from the taxman is your principal residence. Even when individuals create a family trust to hold cottage property, the proposed changes in the last budget would tax the gain when the second spouse dies. The principal residence jumps out as the only opportunity to shelter capital gains once again.

In addition, every family will need to capitalize on every available tax-planning benefit that your home offers to you. The creation of a modest home business would make a portion of your operating expenses associated with your home (i.e., insurance, heat, light, property taxes, water, mortgage interest, etc.) which are normally nondeductible now tax deductible against income generated by your business.

Let's say you convert one room in your six-room house into an office for your business; then, up to one-sixth of the aggregate expenses of your house can become deductible. What's more, if the expenses are even greater than the income derived from your home business, then the differential can be claimed against future income from your home business over the next seven years.

I do not recommend claiming capital cost allowance on the house as it will result in a taxable recapture at the time of resale, which is what we are trying to avoid.

In addition, the house as a tangible collateral can be used as a basis of investment leveraging. Home equity lines of credit can be obtained at prime rates producing interest expenses that are fully tax deductible. This adds further to the resale value of the home.

First-time home buyers have the benefit of RRSP contributions and deductions as well as the right to use up to $20,000 from an RRSP for a contribution towards a downpayment on a house. The RRSP contributions remain deductible in the year they are made, even if withdrawn within 90 days for this purpose.

As the average home buyer in the 1990s will be older and less mobile than home buyers in the 1980s, the average holding period for homes will be between 10 and 15 years. This is, therefore, well into the next residential housing value cycle so that the tax-free capital gains can be realized.

The principal residence will then become a useful component of the retirement income plan. It will allow for the establishment of a systematic withdrawal plan instead of a reverse mortgage. The plan will use the house as collateral which will be kept intact as an asset and not consumed, as is the case with a reverse mortgage.

If we aggregate all these advantages, the principal residence is both a useful quality of family life asset as well as a productive component of a personal financial investment plan.

The Budget and You! A Double Bonus for First-Time Home Buyers

The real estate industry was hoping for an extension of the Home Buyer's Program which allowed first-time home buyers to use up to $20,000 per person from their RRSP holdings toward a first home purchase. What the industry and home buyers received was beyond anyone's expectations.

Effective March 2, 1994, first-time home buyers will be defined as anyone who has not owned a home in the past five years. Contributions made to RRSPs will not only be allowed to be directed toward a home purchase, but the contribution itself made 90 days prior to withdrawal will be allowed as an RRSP deduction as well. This is a double bonus to first-time home buyers — you can buy a home and claim the RRSP contribution as well!

This means that every first-time buyer should flow their new home deposit through an RRSP. The tax savings will add to the return on your home purchase and the cash refund on the taxes actually paid will provide you with extra cash flow to pay down your mortgage when you receive your tax refund.

But Ontario and British Columbia residents have an even better option for 1994. I have talked about the benefits associated with the labour-sponsored venture capital corporation, Integrated Growth Fund or the Active Communications Growth Fund. They allow for government tax credits of up to 40 per cent of your original investment, and the full investment qualifies for your RRSP.

If we assume a first-time home buyer has an RRSP with cash, an attractive investment plan would be as follows:

1) Contribute $10,000 in 1994 to your RRSP ($5,000 in mutual funds and $5,000 in the Integrated Growth Fund or Active Communications Growth Fund).

2) Withdraw $10,000 from your RRSP and apply it toward the downpayment on a home.

3) You will receive up to $2,000 in federal and provincial government tax credits (based on your $5,000 Integrated Growth Fund investment or Active Communications Growth Fund).

4) You will receive roughly $5,000 in tax refunds (assuming a 50 per cent tax bracket).

The end result is that the investor will be able to obtain roughly $7,000 in cash refunds which can then also be applied toward mortgage repayments.

If each spouse did this and was in a similar tax bracket, the family would obtain $14,000 in extra tax-free dollars to pay down the mortgage when they file their tax return in 1995. They can also recontribute the refunds into their RRSP to hasten the repayment.

If they have reasonable credit ratings, they should be able to borrow at least part, if not all of, the contribution. The $14,000 figure is an ideal number. The benefit to the average first-time home buyer if both spouses are working will be in the $10,000 to $12,000 range, but what a bonus and opportunity as well as a savings.

The refunds will save $30,000 to $40,000 in nondeductible interest and greatly enhance the return on investment of the home. Many people 50-plus years of age who sold their homes five years ago or more should now consider purchasing a condominium instead of renting if they are working, are under 71 years of age and have taxable income. This model works identically for them. As they are likely to have higher incomes than first-time buyers in their 20s and 30s, they will benefit from a tax recovery perspective even more.

REAL ESTATE INVESTMENT TRUSTS COME TO CANADA

Real estate investment trusts were started in Canada in the early 1980s with less than stellar results. They were also very popular in the United States in the mid-1980s. These investments allowed investors to participate in what might be considered a mutual fund of buildings which provided both a cash flow return plus capital gains potential.

However, high sales fees, excessive management charges, property management costs, high interest rates and falling real estate values all adversely affected the returns these trusts provided after 1988 and contributed to a loss of consumer confidence. The bloom had come off the rose.

A real estate investment trust (REIT) is a closed-end fund that contains a collection of buildings, usually commercial and industrial, or is in the process of raising money to buy real estate. The purchaser buys a unit in a trust from a licensed stockbroker or financial planner just as they would any mutual fund.

The unit lets you participate in the earnings of land ownership of real estate held by the trust. As the trust is a closed-end fund, it has a limited number of units available, and it is listed on the stock exchange where market factors determine its price and not just its earnings. It gives you easy liquidity and a regular market price for your holdings.

The risk of a trust is determined by the type and quality of the real estate assets held, the amount of debt the trust holds to finance its acquisitions, and its cost of funds.

Income flows from the trust to the unit holders. This income is sheltered by capital cost allowance (depreciation) on the buildings. The trust usually should distribute all of its earnings to the investor. Cash shortfalls can be a problem if the buildings in the trust are not fully occupied or if major tenants leave.

In 1991, these REITs began to experience a recovery. Commercial real estate and strip malls were available at bargain prices and interest rates were at 10-year lows. The opportunities for growth and superior returns were exceptional. The result is that more than $19-billion worth of REITs have been sold in the past two years in the United States. Obviously, investors are still enamored with real estate that could be a bargain.

In January 1994, REITs began to reappear in Canada. Today the situation may be different. Their appearance has been spurred on by the same factors as in the United States — over 30-year lows in interest rates in this country and bargain prices for major commercial building portfolios, strip malls and plazas, and even hotels. This year, 10 to 13 REITs will be offered to private investors and over $1 billion is expected to be raised in Canada for this new type of equity investment.

Many of these investors, put off by poor returns on GICs and a confusing stock market, are being attracted to REITs because of the possibility of participating in real estate bargains that also offer a degree of liquidity. Low real estate prices add sharply to the return potential of the properties and ensure lower break-even points to produce positive cash flow. Low interest rates directly affect investment yields. As many of these new unit buyers are borrowing to invest, the ability to fund larger unit purchases is greatly enhanced, which thereby enhances the appeal of REITs. Also, management records can be more carefully scrutinized and monitored and all offerings are by prospectus only.

In assessing whether a REIT is right for your portfolio, contact your investment advisor and review several prospectuses. Get good independent advice when making a judgement about the ability of the REIT management team, the quality of the properties, estimates of probable returns and the location and type of real estate.

About 19,000 units have been sold in these trusts. In light of the sharp rise in interest rates and decline in the stock market, many investors are looking for a conservative place to park their money. Therefore, there are many questions being raised by new investors about REITs.

A number of new REITs have been formed since January. Some are older real estate mutual funds which were open-ended funds. They are now being converted into REITs.

In making a decision to invest in a REIT, and there are several to choose from, look at who is managing the trust, where the buildings are, what type of buildings are held or will be bought, the management fee, the proposed cost of financing, and the personal tax implications and risk for yourself. Get a prospectus and independent financial advice before you act. A number of REITs have been withdrawn from sale in the past months as brokers felt they were poorly packaged and the real estate overpriced.

While I agree it can be a conservative investment for a more sophisticated investor, for most it should be treated as a new product worthy of careful scrutiny.

CHAPTER SEVEN

Insurance

C learly the Conservative Investor is well-insured with the properly priced products to preserve assets and ensure income protection for the family.

Insurance is of two types: term and permanent. In Canada, there are 148 companies fighting over this market. The volume of insurance sold as an investment has been in decline for some time. Consumers became more knowledgeable and moved their funds into mutual funds and equities as well as more diversified portfolios.

The industry took exceptional losses in the early part of the decade in real estate. Many firms became insolvent and others produced substantial declines in earnings.

To reposition the industry, insurers moved to more innovative products with better returns. Segregated funds, the insurance industry's version of mutual funds, are being heavily promoted. Some have had good returns. All real estate and mortgage-backed investments declined sharply.

Innovative products are of particular relevance to those with high incomes and those with substantial estates.

I have long felt that universal life was undervalued and poorly sold. It is a valuable product to protect insurance coverage if you happen to have a volatile cash flow or unpredictable employment. The investment portion of universal, if adequately financed and properly invested, should after three to five years be adequate to pay the term insurance premiums of the policy.

Returns of quality universal life, if properly invested, should prove to be above average if expenses and fees are carefully monitored and you know what you have bought. The biggest problem is that most people do not understand insurance and its many names and amusing terms. Insurance industry people do themselves and their customers a major disservice by not simplifying policy language and explaining the costs and benefits in simple models.

The marketing of insurance is antiquated and unimaginative. Insurance agents sometimes even find it necessary to call themselves "financial planners" to mask their fear that when the public hears that they offer insurance, they will run screaming from the room.

Term insurance, if properly shopped for, is by far the most affordable of products. There is no savings or investment component involved. You buy it to cover the loss of income of a wage earner and nothing more.

The price variance of the insurance can be as much as 20 per cent or more from company to company. They are confident the consumer is lazy and won't shop the rates. If they feel you really don't understand what you need, they will then promote permanent insurance to you.

Permanent insurance should be bought from a blue chip insurer that is rock solid and carefully and conservatively managed. If it is, say, 20 per cent of your insurance package, then on death there will be an investment component that will provide an estate and pay off capital gains taxes on the estate. Revise your insurance coverage plan every three years.

It is imperative to avoid special "features" in permanent. Avoid such options as accidental death, guaranteed insurability and disability waiver. They all sound great in principal but they are very expensive and not worth the cost of the lost return on your money.

TAX ISSUES

For those in a higher tax bracket who have used up the RRSP contribution limits, universal life allows you to shelter income until the policy pays off on demise.

Investment components of various types of policies produce income that is tax exempt. Any amount paid on the death of the policy owner from the exempt policy is also completely tax exempt. It is a tax- free shelter.

To be an exempt policy, there are clear rules that specify the relationship between the pure insurance component and the investment element. A portion of the total premium must go for pure insurance. It is therefore imperative that you be sure you have purchased an exempt policy.

This type of insurance can be used to

- make charitable donations as a tax credit if you assign the policy to a charity or pay for a policy on their behalf that is owned by you;
- fund supplementary retirement benefits;
- pay a corporate buy-sell arrangement if your private company pays your premium and owns the policy on your life. Proceeds received from the policy will increase the company's capital dividend account and can be paid out tax-free as a dividend to the other corporation's shareholders such as your spouse or children.

There is some disagreement as to whether the tax-exempt component can be attached by creditors or is bullet-proof from them. The same argument applies to RRSP holdings with insurers. Some provinces have argued that they should be attachable, and the issue is still not totally resolved.

Any funds borrowed against a policies and cash surrender value either by using the policy value as collateral or as a loan from the insurance policy will only be treated as income if it is not repaid.

INSURANCE

Insurance Costs and Benefits

No one likes to buy insurance. It is not one of life's great pleasures. It consumes a substantially large portion of our cash and we seem to get very little for it. Yet in this society we must have it.

We spend money on house and liability insurance to protect ourselves from major losses from fire and theft, or against being sued if someone were to have an accident on our property. We insure ourselves against major damages if a pipe breaks in the winter or a tree falls on our house during a storm. At these times household insurance seems a bargain. As part of overall financial planning, insurance is a key element. Every asset, including ourselves, must be insured against loss or damage. We also insure household effects and cars.

Many homeowners would rarely buy as much insurance if they did not have a mortgage that required insurance to protect the lender's interest. We rarely shop our insurance and simply send out a cheque when the annual invoice comes in. Rates should be shopped to three different insurance providers at least every three years. Renters need contents and liability insurance as a basic necessity yet it is estimated that less than 50 per cent of Canadian renters have it.

The same applies to car insurance. There are special rates for abstainers, and those with a clear driving record. Most of us will check these rates because we seem to be more car conscious than home conscious.

Life Insurance

Life insurance is unfortunately not well understood. This is because many people got their first insurance from an employer without charge. While Canadians are the most insured people per capita in the Western world and second only to the Japanese in the G-7, in many cases, Canadians are still underinsured.

Traditionally in the 1950s, '60s and '70s, we bought whole life policies as a so-called forced savings strategy. These were poor investments and expensive insurance coverage. Then, in the 1980s, we moved to universal life that combined term insurance with an investment component that was particularly good for those with volatile incomes such as real estate agents.

Now governments have gone after employer-provided insurance benefits as a taxable income. However, most employer-supplied term insurance, while reasonably priced, is inadequate coverage at three times earnings. Term insurance is the focus of insurance in the 1990s. It is essential to protect the family against catastrophic loss if the principal income earner dies. No one not earning income should be insured. This includes children and non-working spouses. Seniors need insurance to cover death expenses and possible capital gains taxes on estates.

You may need more term life. The old rule was 10 times salary; that is, if you earn $50,000 a year, you need $500,000 in life insurance to provide the same lifestyle and cash flow for the family. With today's lower investment rates on fixed-income holdings, a better rule is 12 to 14 times earnings.

For best results, contact an independent insurance agent and properly plan your insurance as you do your other investments.

TERM INSURANCE

	GENERAL DESCRIPTION	INVESTMENT	INVESTMENT FLEXIBILITY	PREMIUM FLEXIBILITY	FACE AMOUNT FLEXIBILITY
Non-Guaranteed Term	Low Cost	None	N/A	None	None
Yearly Renewable and Convertible Term	Higher Cost	None	N/A	None	None

PERMANENT INSURANCE

	GENERAL DESCRIPTION	INVESTMENT	INVESTMENT FLEXIBILITY	PREMIUM FLEXIBILITY	FACE AMOUNT FLEXIBILITY
Whole Life	Dividends Provide Investment Return. Tax Ameliorated.	Insurance Company Long-Term Bonds and Mortgages	None	None	None
Variable Life	You Direct the Investment	Common Stock, Money Market, etc.	Maximum	None	None
Universal Life	Current Interest Rates	Short-Term Interest Investments	None	Maximum	Maximum
Universal Variable Life	Control Disclosure	Equities, Money Market, etc.	Maximum	Maximum	Maximum

Therefore, the structure of your total insurance should include:

1) Homeowner insurance or renter's insurance.

2) Car and public liability insurance.

3) Disability, especially if self-employed.

4) Term to cover loss of income to the family for wage earners as well as to pay for funeral costs and probate fees.

5) Some permanent life (20 per cent) to cover capital gains on demise. Universal life for individuals with volatile incomes with peaks and valleys. All policies are reviewed and shopped to at least three providers every three years or in the event of a major change in status such as marriage, divorce, new beneficiaries and retirement.

On retirement, the exempt components may be enhanced to beef up the additional contributions above the RRSP. Corporate insurance for closely held companies with company as a beneficiary are ideal for family businesses.

Life insurance is essential to all estate planning to

1) fund the succession or buyout in a closely held business.

2) pay the capital gains taxes on the estate.

3) provide income replacement to children and pay educational costs.

4) cover final expenses such as funerals.

Term insurance is beneficial because of its low cost but gets expensive as you age. Most policies terminate at age 70 or 75.

Permanent insurance is usually at a fixed premium and can be extended to death.

For estate purposes, if the policy is paid to the estate, it will be used to meet creditor claims and probate fees. A more beneficial route is to pay it to family members or the spouse. You'll want all policies to have a designated beneficiary if they are permanent ones as the cash surrender value or investment component may be protected from creditors as a result.

While in principle we can protect the insurance from probate fees by making the beneficiary a trust, there are limitations when the beneficiaries are minors, if the proceeds are governed by your will, or the beneficiary dies at the same time as the insured.

A proper estate insurance declaration as part of your estate plan will cover this situation.

CHAPTER EIGHT

A Conservative Retirement Plan

The essence of planning for retirement is to ensure you have adequate income to maintain the lifestyle you want, where you want and for as long as you want.

The strategy to achieve this must be based on establishing an income stream for your retirement years of 70 per cent to 75 per cent of your best five years of earnings. This is based on the fact that you probably will have multiple sources of income, some under your control and others under government control. The bad news is that the government intends to expand its sphere of influence and maximize its tax grab.

When you retire, income will come from:

1) Personal savings and investments.

2) Income from a company pension plan.

3) RRSP income as an annuity or payments from a Registered Retirement Income Fund.

4) Proceeds from a Registered Pension Plan annuity which you can maximize and control.

5) Canada Pension Plan or Quebec Old Age Security (minus the clawback) which are under government control.

Figure 8.1: How Much You Need to Save Each Year for Retirement

Step No. 1
Decide what percentage of your annual salary you will need in retirement, on top of traditional company pension, if any, and CPP. Then use this table to find the percentage of salary you need to save each year, depending on how long you have until retirement.

DESIRED RETIREE INCOME AS A % OF ANNUAL SALARY

| | Years to Retirement | | | | | |
	10	15	20	25	30	35
30%	36%	21%	13%	9%	6%	4%
40%	48	27	18	12	8	6
50%	60	34	22	15	10	7
60%	72	41	26	18	12	9
70%	84	48	31	21	14	10

Step No. 2
Adjust the required savings rate to take account of your current savings by finding the appropriate number in this table and subtracting it from the percentage determined in Step 1.

CURRENT SAVINGS AS A % OF ANNUAL SALARY YEARS TO RETIREMENT

| | Years to Retirement | | | | | |
Savings	10	15	20	25	30	35
100%	13%	10%	8%	7%	7%	6%
200%	25	19	16	14	13	13
300%	38	29	24	22	20	19
400%	51	38	32	29	27	25
500%	64	48	40	36	33	32

Example: If you are 25 years from retirement and want a retirement income equal to 70% of your salary, the first table suggests you need to save 21% a year. But if you already have savings equal to 200% of your salary, you would reduce that number by 14 to get a 7% annual savings rate.

THE BENEFITS OF CONTRIBUTING TO AN RRSP ARE OVERWHELMING

Table 8.1: Future Value of a $1,000 Investment in a GIC after Tax

YEARS	6%	8%	10%	12%	14%	16%
1	1,028	1,038	1,047	1,056	1,066	1,075
5	1,149	1,203	1,258	1,316	1,375	1,437
10	1,321	1,445	1,583	1,731	1,891	2,065
15	1,518	1,740	1,992	2,277	2,601	2,967
20	1,744	2,092	2,506	2,996	3,577	4,264
25	2,004	2,516	3,153	3,942	4,919	6,127
30	2,303	3,026	3,966	5,186	6,765	8,804
35	2,647	3,640	4,990	6,823	9,304	12,651

Table 8.2: Future Value of a $1,000 Invstment in RRSPs

YEARS	6%	8%	10%	12%	14%	16%
1	1,060	1,080	1,100	1,120	1,140	1,160
5	1,338	1,469	1,611	1,762	1,925	2,100
10	1,791	2,159	2,594	3,106	3,707	4,411
15	2,397	3,172	4,177	5,474	7,138	9,266
20	3,207	4,661	6,727	9,646	13,743	19,461
25	4,292	6,848	10,835	17,000	26,462	40,874
30	5,743	10,063	17,449	29,960	50,950	85,850
35	7,686	14,785	28,102	52,800	98,100	180,314

Assumption: the marginal tax rate is 53%.

Yet the latest research shows that for 1992:

- Only 34.7 per cent of households made an RRSP contribution.
- The average contribution was $950.
- Of those with incomes over $90,000, 75 per cent made a contribution averaging $4,800.
- Only 20.3 per cent of female tax filers made an RRSP contribution.
- Those under age 30 represent 15 per cent of contributors.

The retirement assets are:

- 65 per cent in Registered Pension Plans

- 24 per cent in RRSPs
- 11 per cent in CPP

Where do the returns actually come from?

1949-1993 Historical Average Returns
Treasury Bills	6.3%
Canadian Savings Bonds	8.3%
Canadian Stocks	10.8%
Inflation Average	4.5%

A Balanced Portfolio:
50 per cent equities; 40 per cent bonds; 10 per cent cash.

The Saving

If you save $2,000 a year before tax and invest your RRSP to earn only 8 per cent at a tax rate of 40 per cent over 30 years, you would have $244,692.

Table 8.3: Savings by Province

How much can be saved for every $1,000 RRSP contribution deducted if you are taxed at the top rate? With higher provincial taxes and surtaxes, the tax break offered by RRSPs is much greater in some provinces than in others.

Quebec	$529
Ontario	$523
Saskatchewan	$519
Newfoundland	$513
British Columbia	$511
New Brunswick	$507
Manitoba	$504
Prince Edward Island	$503
Nova Scotia	$503
Yukon	$465
Alberta	$461
Northwest Territories	$444

The following is the eligible list for 1994 for self- directed RRSPs.

1) Cash.
2) Canadian guaranteed investment certificates and term deposits.
3) Canadian dollar deposits in a bank, trust company or credit union.
4) Mutual funds registered with Revenue Canada.

5) Shares, rights, warrants and call options listed on the Montreal, Toronto, Winnipeg, Alberta and Vancouver stock exchanges or the Toronto Futures Exchange. Unlisted Canadian public corporations also qualify.

6) Shares on eligible foreign exchanges. Warrants and rights held on these shares are also eligible:

   • United States: the American, New York, Boston, Chicago, Cincinnati, Detroit, Midwest, National, Pacific, Pittsburgh, Salt Lake, Philadelphia-Baltimore-Washington, Spokane and NASDAQ.
   • Europe: Amsterdam, Brussels, Frankfurt, London, Madrid, Milan, Paris and Zurich.
   • Other: Australia, Hong Kong, Mexico, New Zealand and Singapore.

7) Bonds (including Canada Savings Bonds) and other debt instruments guaranteed by the Government of Canada, a province, municipality, or Crown corporation. Included are those issued in foreign currency.

8) Bonds and debentures issued by a corporation trading on a Canadian stock exchange.

9) Debt instruments issued by public corporations not listed on Canadian stock exchanges.

10) Foreign bonds and debentures of corporations whose shares are listed on a prescribed foreign stock exchange.

11) Debt instruments of foreign governments, which at the time of purchase have an investment grade rating.

12) Stripped versions of eligible bonds are also eligible.

13) Closed-end funds.

14) A mortgage on real Canadian property (including your own house if certain conditions are met).

15) Mortgage-backed securities.

16) Some life insurance policies.

17) Life annuities with guaranteed terms of less than 15 years.

18) Share of a credit union.

19) Shares of a small business corporation to a limit of 50 per cent of your RRSP.

20) Shares in a labour-sponsored venture capital corporation, unless you live in Alberta, New Brunswick or Newfoundland.

21) Bankers' acceptances.

22) Limited partnership units listed on a Canadian stock exchange. Counted as foreign property within your RRSP unless they are small business investment limited partnerships.

THE NEW RRSP CHANGES TO BE AWARE OF

The Foreign Content Limit of RRSPs

This increased to 20 per cent in 1994 from 18 per cent in 1993. The percentage refers to the book value — the original cost of your investments — and not the current market value.

Who Is the Spouse?

The term spouse now applies both to a legally married husband or wife and a common-law spouse. A common-law spouse is a person of the opposite sex who, at that particular time:

- Was living with you in a common-law relationship and is the natural or adoptive parent of your child, or
- Was living with you in a common-law relationship and had been living with you for at least 12 continuous months.

This means that you can now set up a spousal RRSP for your common-law spouse. In addition, if you die, your RRSP or registered retirement income fund can be transferred to your common-law spouse's RRSP or RRIF tax free.

Membership in a Foreign Pension Plan

If you participated in a foreign pension plan in 1993, you may have a pension adjustment for 1993, and as a result, your 1994 RRSP deduction limit may be reduced. Similarly, if you participated in a foreign plan and your past-service benefit accruing under this plan was increased in 1994, you may have a net past service pension adjustment for 1994 and, as a result, your 1994 RRSP deduction limit may be reduced.

These two changes take away some advantages for people who have foreign pension plans and put them on a more equal footing with people with Canadian plans. Previously, for example, those working temporarily in Canada for a foreign company could make maximum RRSP tax-free contributions because their accrued foreign-pension benefits were not considered. When they left Canada, they could get their RRSP money out at a very low tax rate.

New Eligible RRSP Investments

The following are new RRSP, RRI and deferred profit-sharing plan qualified investments:

- Certain warrants and bankers' acceptances.
- Limited partnership units listed on a Canadian stock exchange. These are counted as foreign property within your RRSP unless they are exempt, as are small business investment limited partnerships.

- Debt obligations issued by public corporations not listed on Canadian stock exchanges.

- Debt obligations (for example, bonds and debentures) acquired after June 21, 1993, of corporations whose shares are listed on a prescribed foreign stock exchange.

- Debt obligations acquired after June 21, 1993, of foreign governments, which at the time of purchase have an investment grade rating with a bond rating agency that ordinarily rates debt issued by foreign governments (foreign content).

Home Buyer's Plan

As described in our real estate section, the new rules extend the plan in perpetuity and reclassify the first-time home buyer as anyone who hasn't bought a home in five years. And long as the RRSP contribution is in place 90 days prior to withdrawal, you still get the RRSP deduction.

Transfers to Dependent Child or Grandchild

If there is no spouse when an RRSP or RRIF holder dies, you can transfer the contents to a financially dependent child or grandchild who can then buy an annuity to age 18. However, if the child is dependent because of mental or physical disability, there is no age restriction and in this case the money can buy an annuity, or be transferred to the child's RRIF or RRSP. Starting with the 1993 tax year, however, in both cases the child must generally have had an income under $6,456 in 1992. That limit will be increased with inflation at the same rate as the personal exemption.

Saskatchewan Pension Plan

New rules apply to money received from the SPP. It must be transferred directly from the SPP to an RRSP or RRIF for it to be a tax-free contribution. Previously, the transfer did not have to be direct.

Revamped Revenue Canada Guide

The RRSP guide is now called *RRSP and Other Registered Plans for Retirement*, changed from *Pension and RRSP Tax Guide*.

Figure 8.2.

SELF-DIRECTED RETIREMENT SAVINGS PLANS

Institution	Annual admin. fees	Transaction fees	Transfer/ closing fees	Mutual funds/options	Mortgage admin. fees
Bank of Montreal	$100	$20; free if company sponsored broker	$50; none if transferred internally. Withdrawal $25	Allowed	$225 a year and $150 set-up fee
Bank of Nova Scotia	$100	None	$50; none if transferred internally	Allowed	$175 a year and $100 set-up fee
Laurentian Bank	$100 + $50 for dividend reinvestment	None $10 NASDAQ $75 EUROCLEAR $10 External GIC/RSP	Withdrawal/ transfer $50. No charge if internal	Mutual funds only	$150 annual fee
Manulife Bank	$150	$15. 10 free	None	Allowed	$150 annual fee $100–$250 set-up fee
National Bank	$100	None $25 cash wd.	Transfer $50; de-registration $50	Allowed	Not allowed
Toronto-Dominion Bank	$100; $25 if holding only Green Line funds	None, except SWAPS $45	Full transfer $50. Partial wd. or transfer $25	Allowed Only options are covered calls	$200 a year $100 set-up fee
Canada Trust	$100	None	External transfer $25; partial wd. $25; $100 if open less than 6 months, one free per year	Mutual funds only	$200 a year $150 set-up fee
Montreal Trust	$200, fee reduced to $75 if holding $100,000 in Montreal Trust products	$15 None if using company sponsored program	$50 full transfer; de-registration $50	Allowed. Only options are covered calls	$200 a year $200 set-up fee
National Trust	$125	$15; first 4 free; National products free	$50 transfer or wd.; $50 closing fee; $25 partial transfer or wd.	Allowed. Only options are covered calls	$200 a year and minimum $100 set-up
North American Trust	$100 $50 if holding only CSBs	None	$100 transfer or wd.; $25 partial de-registration	Allowed. Only options are covered calls	$175–$225 a year $250 set-up fee
Royal Trust	$100	None $25 non RT GICs	$50	Mutual funds only	$275 a year $100 set-up fee
Burns Fry	$125 pro-rated	None	$100 Closing. $25 Partial	Allowed. Only options are covered calls	$175 a year and $200 set-up fee
CIBC Securities	$100	None	$50	Allowed	$150 a year $100 set-up fee
First Marathon	$110	None	None	Allowed. Only options are covered calls	Not allowed

Institution	Annual admin. fees	Transaction fees	Transfer/ closing fees	Mutual funds/options	Mortgage admin. fees
Midland Walwyn	$125	None	$50 de-registration Partial wd $25 to max. $100. Thereafter $50	Allowed. Only options are covered calls	$200 a year and $200 set-up fee
Nesbitt Thompson	$125 $75 locked in funds	None	$100 full transfer. $50 full wd. $25 partial wd.	Allowed. Only options are covered calls	Not allowed $100 set-up fee
RBC Dominion Securities	$116.82	None	$100. Partial transfer $25. Full wd. $50	Allowed. Only options are covered calls	$175 a year and $100 set-up fee
Royal Bank Investor Tranding Inc.	$100	None	$25	Mutual funds only	Not allowed
Richardson Greenshields	$125 pro-rated	None	$100	Allowed. Only options are Cdn. covered calls	$50 annual fee $100 set-up fee
Scotia Discount Brokerage	$75	None	$50 full transfer wd.; $15 partial	Allowed. Only options are covered calls	$175 annual fee $175 set-up fee
Scotia McLeod	$120, but $60 if client is over 60	None	$100. Partial $15.	Allowed.	$175 annual fee $100 set-up fee
Wood Gundy	$125	None	$50 de-registration; $50 full transfer; partial $25	Allowed. Only options are covered calls	$175 annual fee $175 set-up fee

Transaction fees do not include brokerage fees. Mortgage set-up fees are usually associated with non-arm's length mortgages. Mortgage administration fees do not include renewal, discharge, appraisal, mortgage insurance or legal fees.

BASIC CONSERVATIVE RRSP STRATEGIES

1) Maximize your foreign content: only 22 per cent of RRSP contributors have foreign content in their self-directed RRSP.

2) Establish a monthly contribution plan to insure you maximize from the beginning of the year.

3) If you don't have cash to contribute, then contribute other assets such as real estate and equities.

4) Break the GIC habit — there are other and better options. Look at the list.

5) Make sure you have a spousal plan for income splitting on retirement. The elimination of the age exemption, OAP clawback and other reductions of the maximum income levels and penalties for diligence, mean that income splitting is an absolute must.

6) Never miss a contribution, ever.

7) If you contribute early in the year, each year you can add 10 per cent to the value of your RRSP over your contribution period.

8) Get your children contributing from 18 onwards.

9) Let the government know you have maximized your contribution early and reduce withholding tax at source by your employer.

10) Consolidate your RRSP holdings to save administrative fees and maximize returns.

11) It is realistic for a high-net-worth individual to borrow to invest in your RRSP. Pay off the debt quickly.

12) Over-contribute the $8,000 while you can.

13) Maximize your earned income for your RRSP qualification to maximize your RRSP.

14) When an employee retires at normal retirement age or is terminated before then, it is not uncommon for the employer to pay a retirement allowance. This was very common for early retirees or those severed after 20 to 30 years of employment. $2,000 per year of a retirement allowance can be transferred to an RRSP for each year of service and an additional $1,500 per year of service prior to 1989 if you were not a member of a registered pension plan. The investment is placed directly into the RRSP and there is no withholding tax.

BULLET-PROOFING YOUR RRSP

Employer-sponsored registered pension plans are protected from creditors as are locked-in RRSPs and life income funds (LIFs) that hold pension plan money. It can be attacked by an ex-spouse.

Revenue Canada has been successful of late in pursuing a case against the income from a pension plan to an individual, but not the capital.

RRSPs and RRIFs from life insurance companies may be protected if the following conditions apply:

1) There is a named beneficiary such as a child, grandchild, parent or spouse.

2) If anyone who is not a family member is named they must be an irrevocable beneficiary.

3) You are not in difficulty financially when you make the RRSP contribution. If you go bankrupt in one year, the plan can be attacked.

4) It must be an insurance RRSP or RRIF that is an insurance contract, including GIC deposits and "segregated" insurance company mutual funds.

5) Three provinces have extended protection:

> P.E.I.: All RRSPs and RRIFs are protected subject to the conditions above.
> B.C.: Grants credit proofing at death for all RRSPs and RRIFs if the designated beneficiary was irrevocable.

Quebec: Provincially chartered trust companies can offer RRSP and RRIF fixed term deposit annuities that are bullet-proofed.

RRIF — REGISTERED RETIREMENT INCOME FUNDS

The rules have changed and you will be much more heavily taxed in the first seven years of your RRIF.

Figure 8.3: Assumptions

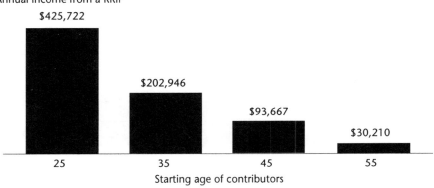

- Maximum RRSP contribution until age 65, and then none until age 71
- RRIF payments start at age 72
- RRIF used up by age 91
- 7% interest rate
- No increase in maximum beyond $15,500

Annual income from a RRIF

- $425,722 — 25
- $202,946 — 35
- $93,667 — 45
- $30,210 — 55

Starting age of contributors

All RRIF plans are not the same. You can have several different types, including GIC, mutual funds, guaranteed annuities and self-directed or managed plans.

Make sure you pay your RRIF administration fees outside your plan to ensure their deductibility. Designate a beneficiary in your will as well as in all plan documents to protect the plan from probate fees and taxes. You will need real growth investments in the plan if you are in good health. This means more than GICs. You may need yields of 9 per cent to 11 per cent or more to maintain your lifestyle.

You can withdraw RRIF income monthly or even annually at year-end earnings tax sheltered returns. The goal is to customize the income stream to meet your needs, to reduce taxes and to maximize allowance deductions.

It is not excessively difficult or complex. Remember to spend non-tax-sheltered money first, then start RRIF income when this is exhausted.

OTHER INVESTMENTS AND THEIR RISK RATINGS

TYPE	TREND	RISK
Baseball and Hockey Cards	Going nowhere	High
Sports Collectibles	Only 5-10% are any good; the rest is going down	High
First Edition and Antique Books	Upward	Moderate
Coins — Gold, not ancient	Quality is everything	Moderate
Comic Books	Too many copies	High
Movie Posters	Hot	Moderate
Antique Toys & Teddy Bears	Hot	Moderate
Paperweights	Hot	High
Silver — Antique	Georgian is forever	Moderate
Animation	Disney's everywhere; too many	High
Antique Jewellery	Designer Quality is hot	Moderate
Antique Furniture	Quiet for many years and now up	Moderate
Art Glass	Gallé, Tiffany — crashed	High
Pre-1867 Canadian Furniture	Will live forever — upward	Moderate

CHAPTER NINE

Estate Planning

E state planning is one of the cornerstones of a sound financial plan. Essentially, the purpose of an estate plan is to preserve your wealth both during your lifetime and after. What you do today can make a world of difference to your happiness and the future of people you care about most.

Here are some of the basic questions to be addressed.

Will my spouse inherit everything — even if I don't leave a will?

If you were to die without proper estate planning, your assets would be distributed according to intestacy laws. In Ontario, for example, the first $75,000 of your estate would go to your spouse as a preferential share. If you have no children, the portion of your estate remaining after the preferential share would also go to your spouse. However, debts will be charged on the assets of the estate so the total value of your estate may be reduced significantly by creditors. Your spouse may therefore receive less than you have contemplated.

If you leave a spouse and one child, that child will be entitled to one-half of the residue left after the $75,000 preferential share to your spouse. Your spouse will be entitled to the other half. If you have more than one child, your spouse will be entitled to only one-third of the residue. The remaining two-thirds will be divided equally among the children.

This division could leave your spouse with insufficient funds to live on. Should your spouse be forced to sell assets, he or she may be liable for significant capital taxes that proper estate planning could have deferred until spouse's death. We can put non-taxable term insurance in place to pay all this tax.

In addition, the administration of the courts take a great deal of extra time.

Will my children be provided for?

The full benefits that you would have intended your children to have during their growing years may be lost. The portion of the estate which passes to any child who is under 18 will not be immediately released to your spouse for the child's benefit. This portion will be paid into court and held until the child becomes of age. A court will give an order to pay all or a portion of any money belonging to your child, or the income from the property, to your child's guardian, only if satisfied that it is necessary or proper for the support or education of the child, or that it would substantially benefit the child. This is a time-consuming and costly process. If the Provincial Trustee is involved, expect the situation to become a problem.

Does a will restrict my assets?

A will places no type of encumbrance on any type of asset until after your death. The will's existence and contents may be kept strictly confidential during your lifetime. You may revoke or vary it as often as required. The will becomes operative only on your death.

How can I minimize my income tax liability?

Unlike most Western countries, Canada does not levy estate taxes or succession duties, either federally or provincially. However, income tax will be payable on your death. The amount of income tax payable will depend, to some degree, on the terms of your will and the decisions your executors make. Income received during the year of death is taxable in the same way as during any prior year of your life. Ontario is considering the imposition of estate taxes in their report from the Fair Tax Commission. If it does, Quebec and Ottawa will follow shortly.

What is the status of capital gains?

Your capital assets, even though you didn't sell anything, are deemed to have been sold for fair market value immediately before your death. Thus, capital gains and losses are included in calculating your income tax for that year. This may result in a sizable tax assessment but, because no real sale took place, the proceeds will not be available. Unless your estate plan includes special provisions to cover this tax liability, assets will likely have to be sold to pay this additional income tax. This is where the insurance comes in.

The tax on capital gains be deferred by transferring capital property to your surviving spouse or to a trust that qualifies as a "spousal trust." Gains on property transferred to your spouse or a spousal trust are not taxable during your spouse's lifetime unless the property is sold. To qualify as a spousal trust under the Income Tax Act, your spouse must be entitled to all of the net income from the trust and no one else may be allowed to receive any capital from the trust during your spouse's lifetime.

Capital Losses

If your final income tax return will show substantial capital gains, assets that you expect will yield a capital loss could be transferred to someone other than your spouse by your will. This will avoid the tax-free rollover of the property, and your final tax return will have a capital loss that will be deductible from the capital gains.

Your executor may be able to save your estate some income tax by filing a separate tax return that includes only "Rights and Things." "Rights and Things" may include any payment to which you have a right in the future, such as dividends declared but unpaid, uncashed matured bond coupons and vacation pay not taken. Your personal representative will have the discretion to decide whether to include such things in the standard income tax return, to file a separate return (this provides a second set of deductions and splits the income of the estate), or to transfer the asset to the beneficiary immediately (thus putting the tax burden on the beneficiary).

Probate Costs

Probate fees are the highest in Ontario where they have recently been tripled to 0.5 per cent of the first $50,000 and 1.5 per cent on everything else. Elsewhere in Canada, the fees are 0.3 per cent to 0.6 per cent of the value in estate. Alberta has a $1,000 flat fee and Quebec charges $45.

The probate fee applies to the total value of all assets without any deductions for liabilities other than mortgages on real estate.

Real Estate

One of the traditional ways of avoiding probate fees is to ensure that real estate interests are held in "joint tenancy with right of survivorship." In this way, the interest of joint tenant disappears upon that individual's death, thereby excluding it from the estate so that it is not subject to probate fees.

Alternatively, if you know who is intended to receive a particular piece of real estate upon your death, another option is to transfer title of the property to that person, reserving a life interest for yourself.

Deposits with Banks/Trust Companies

Joint ownership with right of survivorship can also be established for an account of other form of deposit with a bank or trust company, although the amount of the applicable probate fees may not warrant setting up the accounts in this manner.

Since not all joint accounts are subject to the right of survivorship, check the account documents held by your financial institution to determine whether this right applies.

Life Insurance

Life insurance proceeds can also be protected from probate fees. While in principle this is easily accomplished by ensuring that the proceeds are payable to a named individual, there may be problems in circumstances where:

- the beneficiaries are minors
- the insured prefers to have the proceeds governed by his or her will; or
- the insured and the named beneficiary die in common accident.

Inter Vivos Trusts

Setting up an estate plan through a trust established during your lifetime, rather than through a will, can also minimize fees.

ESTATE ADMINISTRATION

In a case where an individual did not take precautions to ensure that his or her assets would pass outside the estate, it may still be possible, upon the individual's death, to administer the estate without paying probate fees. This depends, however, on the nature and value of the assets and the person who has control of them.

Establishing/Reviewing an Estate Plan

Even if an estate plan has been put in place, it should be periodically reviewed. Any review should be made with the following changes in mind:

- relevant legislation
- asset mix
- size of estate
- birth or death of relatives or intended beneficiaries.

An estate plan can be undertaken either during the lifetime of an individual in order to satisfy current financial needs, or by will in order to plan for succession.

If the estate plan is established during the individual's lifetime, the following considerations apply:

- the minimization of income taxes, possibly through income splitting with family members
- for Quebec residents, the eligibility of gift taxes
- the necessity of liquidity
- the potential permanent disability of the individual.

The latter consideration is quite vital should an individual become disabled after establishing an estate plan. Sufficient assets may no longer be available to adequately support the individual. Consequently, an estate plan should be set up in such a manner as to leave the individual with sufficient assets available to overcome unforeseen hardships.

If an estate plan is established by will, the individual can provide for the following:

- the timing of transfers to intended beneficiaries
- the separation of income, capital, and control thereof
- post-mortem tax planning.

Taxation Objectives

An estate plan that is intended to prepare for the eventuality of death must deal with significant income tax effect. At death, the provisions of the Income Tax Act provide a change in emphasis from the normal cash accounting basis that is followed by an individual, to an accrual basis of measuring taxable income. As a general rule, taxes become payable at death on all previously untaxed increments in wealth.

There are, however, certain exceptions, depending upon the relationship of the successor to the deceased and the nature of the assets of the deceased. Consequently, the principal taxation objectives of an estate plan are to reduce and/or defer taxes upon death.

The most common methods used to reduce taxes upon death are as follows:

a) freezing an estate during the lifetime of the individual

b) realizing capital gains during the lifetime of the individual, and

c) making gifts during the lifetime of the individual to reduce the value of the estate at death.

The most common means of deferring taxes upon death are as follows:

a) transferring property to a spouse or spousal trust

b) using certain exceptions to the deemed disposition provisions of the Income Tax Act such as:

- the deferral of up to $500,000 of capital gains arising on the transfer of shares of a small business corporation or family farm where the property is transferred to a child, grandchild, or great-grandchild of the deceased; or
- the transfer at cost from the deceased of farmland and depreciable property used in the business of farming, of shares of a corporation, or of an interest in a partnership that operates a farm.

Generally, it is useful to have an overall estate plan in mind when the will of the individual is being prepared. An overall estate plan helps to ensure that the will provides for an orderly transfer of assets from one generation to another, and because the will designates an executor or trustee, it provides for the competent administration of the estate after the death of the individual. Furthermore, unless an estate plan is properly timed, the value of the estate may be eroded through income taxes being eligible on deemed realizations and, depending upon the residence of the deceased and the sites of any property held, succession duties or foreign estate taxes.

Estate Freezing

The purpose of an estate freeze is to limit the value of some or all of the assets of an individual's estate. Effectively, the value of the assets is fixed at the date of the freeze. Consequently, when the individual dies and the deemed disposition provisions of the Income Tax Act take effect, the tax liability is already fixed.

Even though the individual has fixed the value of the assets comprises his estate by effecting an estate freeze, the individual may still control those assets. It is only the growth in the value of those assets that will accrue to the beneficiaries of the freeze during the individual's lifetime.

An estate freeze is generally structured to avoid any immediate tax cost to the individual. The main benefit of establishing an estate freeze is that the individual can decide who his beneficiaries will be and which assets they will receive. Furthermore, since the estate freeze is a deliberately planned event which serves to fix the value of the individual's estate, the individual knows what his tax liability will be at death and, consequently, is able to determine how that liability will be funded. The funding of the tax liability can be done by determining which assets to keep and which to sell in order to meet that liability upon death. Alternatively, insurance can be purchased to fund it.

Methods

An estate freeze is an individually tailored mechanism. There are several methods that can be used to effect the freeze. However, common to all of the methods used is the notion of exchanging an asset that will increase in value for an asset which will not increase in value. Because the substituted asset will not increase in value, the tax liability on the disposition of that asset will be readily determinable. The three most common methods of effecting an estate freeze are 1) a sale or gift; 2) a trust; 3) a holding company freeze.

The sale or gifting of an asset to the intended beneficiary is the simplest method of freezing an estate. If a gift is used, the value of the estate at death is simply reduced by the value of the gift made during the lifetime of the individual. If, instead, an asset is sold, consideration in the form of demand promissory note could be received in return. All future growth in the value of the asset will accrue to the beneficiary who receives the asset.

There are, however, two problems with this method of estate freezing:

a) the individual loses control of the assets, and

b) the individual has disposed of the asset and will be taxable on any gain.

This may result in a tax liability arising in a situation where the individual has not received cash from the sale. Where the individual makes a gift of the asset, the individual is deemed to have received proceeds of disposition equal to the fair market value of that asset transferred by gift. Accordingly, with both a gift and a sale there may be an immediate income tax liability.

If a trust is used as the mechanism for an estate freeze, the individual either gifts or sells the asset to a trust for the intended beneficiary. There may be a gain and immediate income tax liability at the time of the gifting or the selling of the asset to the trust. Nevertheless, the use of the trust to effect an estate freeze enables the individual to maintain a certain degree of control by means of the selection of the trustees. Since the trust owns the asset, any growth will be for the benefit of the beneficiary.

Should the individual have assets which may include a portfolio of investments, a rental property, or a share of an operating company, a holding company freeze could be utilized. To effect such a freeze, the assets to be frozen would be sold to the corporation. The individual in return would take back a combination of debt and shares from the corporation.

The corporation receiving the assets would be structured so as to have at least two classes of shares: special shares and common shares. The special shares would be specifically designated as no-growth. Any increment in the value of the assets would then be reflected by an increase in the value of the common shares. The individual transferring the assets would receive back the no-growth special shares. Consequently, the value of the individual's assets would be fixed at the date of the freeze. The intended beneficiaries of the estate freeze would subscribe for common shares of the corporation. This will ensure that all growth in the value of the assets will accrue in the hands of the beneficiaries.

In order to accomplish a holding company freeze on a tax-free basis, the individual and the corporation to which he is transferring his assets must jointly elect to have the provisions of Section 85 of the Income Tax Act apply to the transaction. The advantage of this method of estate freezing is the deferral of income tax on the disposition of the assets that are frozen, while maintaining control of those assets through the special shares which can be voting shares.

This method of an estate freeze also enables the individual to maintain a certain cash flow. For example, the individual may receive cash by interest, principal payments on any debt consideration, and dividends on any share consideration. Furthermore, shares may be redeemed to provide an increased cash flow.

WILLS

The importance of a will in the proper planning of one's affairs cannot be underestimated. By means of a will, you can provide for:

1) the distribution of property to the beneficiaries you wish

2) the administration of the estate

3) the appointment of an executor to carry out the administration of the estate.

A will is essential to ensure that property is bequeathed to persons as chosen by the testator. You are the testator. For example, the testator may wish to make certain charitable bequests, or leave sums of money or personal effects to specific persons. Without a will, the deceased's property would be distributed pursuant to a scheme of distribution as set out by statute. Furthermore, a court-appointed representative would attend to the administration of the estate. Consequently, without a will, the result may be far removed from what the wishes of the testator might have been.

The statutory scheme of distribution varies from province to province. However, each provincial statute provides that property passes first to the deceased's spouse and children.

Almost anyone may prepare a will. However some individuals are precluded form doing so, namely

- an individual who has not yet attained the age of majority (18 years in all provinces except Newfoundland, British Columbia, New Brunswick and Nova Scotia), unless the will is prepared in contemplation of marriage; or

- an individual who is not of "sound mind."

There are further general restraints which add that a will must be in writing and must comply with the provincial legislation regarding formalities for signing.

Types of Wills

There are two basic types of will that are most commonly used: a formal will, and an informal will. The formal type of will is the most common and is recognized across Canada. This type of will has certain specific requirements:

- the will must be signed by the testator or by someone in his presence and at his direction

- the testator must make or acknowledge his signature in the presence of at least two witnesses

- two or more witnesses must attest to this fact by also signing the document in the testator's presence

- neither the witnesses nor their spouses must be beneficiaries under the will.

In most provinces in Canada, except British Columbia, Nova Scotia and Prince Edward Island, a more informal type of will is also recognized. The informal type of will is known as a holograph will. A holograph will must also meet certain requirements:

- the entire will must be handwritten

- the will must be signed at the end by the testator

- no witnesses are required.

Revising a Will

It is essential for anyone who has made a will to review it periodically. Generally, the assistance of a professional advisor is helpful, to ensure that changes in circumstances or legislation have not undermined the original intent of the will. Furthermore, if changes are considered necessary at that time, they can then be accomplished quickly.

Changes to a will can be made in two ways depending upon the degree of change. If there are to be deletions to the original document that are major changes, then the will should be revoked and a new will drafted. If there are minor amendments to the will, these can be easily made by using a codicil. A codicil resembles an addition or alteration.

If a codicil is used, it should specifically refer to the original will by date, and then state the required changes. A codicil is subject to the same formalities as the original will, whether conventional or holograph, although the same witnesses are not required.

As indicated, if major amendments to a will are required, it is best to have a completely new will drawn up. This serves to avoid confusion since the old will is specifically revoked. A will may be revoked at any time during the testator's life by the following methods: physically destroying the document, or expressing the intention to revoke the will in a subsequent written document that is formally executed as if it were a will.

In all provinces except Quebec, if a testator marries after making a will, that will is automatically revoked. In Ontario, legislation provides that divorce invalidates certain portions of the former spouse's will. Because of the effect of such legislation, it is important to review and revise a will on a continuing basis. This has been the cause of much litigation.

Important Considerations

Since the will only takes effect upon the death of the testator, it is extremely important to deal with all possible situations at the time of drafting, and to make the will as clear as possible. Some of the more general considerations are as follows:

(i) Assets

Consideration must be given to any future inheritances or dispositions anticipated by the testator. Any assets that will not be automatically included in the testator's estate should be identified as such, since property that is jointly held automatically passes to the survivor. Other assets such as pension plans or other benefit plans which designate a beneficiary need not be dealt with in a will.

(ii) Beneficiaries

The testator must clearly identify whom he intends to benefit. If possible, the beneficiary should be identified by name and description. In naming beneficiaries, a testator has virtually unlimited discretion to benefit or ignore people, dependants being the one significant exception. A dependant is any person whom the testator was in fact supporting or obligated to support. Where inadequate provisions have been made by a deceased for dependants, a dependant can apply to court, and the courts can order a redistribution of the deceased's estate.

(iii) Executors

It is advisable to appoint someone who is younger than the testator and who is willing to act as an executor. More than one executor may be named; in fact, it is frequently advisable to name an alternate executor in the event that the original executor becomes unable or unwilling to act.

(iv) Gifts

A testator may want to leave specific possessions or bequests of money to a particular person or charitable organization. Both the gift and the beneficiary must be described in sufficient detail to enable the executor to carry out the wish of the testator. Consideration must be given to succession duty implications where the property is situated, or if the beneficiary is resident in Quebec.

WILL PROVISIONS

1. Is the will being made in contemplation of marriage?
2. Executors and trustees.
3. Guardians of minors.
4. Registered retirement savings plan, deferred-profit sharing plan, and registered home ownership savings plan designations.
5. Insurance declaration.
6. Specific disposition of articles or ornaments of personal, domestic, and household use.
7. Specific disposition of any other assets.
8. If spouse survives, specific provisions for children.
9. If spouse survives, specific provisions for grandchildren.
10. If spouse survives, specific provisions for parents/parents-in-law.
11. If spouse survives, specific provisions for other beneficiaries, including charity.
12. Provisions for spouse.
13. If trust for spouse, disposition of balance of property on death of spouse, and if spouse predeceases.
14. Disposition on common disaster or failure of trust(s).

15. Circumstances requiring special consideration (e.g., physical or mental disability of a beneficiary).

16. Bequests to charity on subsequent death of spouse or in event of common disaster or failure of trust(s).

17. Are any adopted children to be treated the same as natural children?

18. Dower provision.

19. Should the will contain different dispositive provisions depending on whether testator has received a capital interest in an estate or trust or an expected inheritance?

20. Does testator wish to exercise any power of appointment granted to him under any will or trust agreement? If so, obtain a copy of the document granting the power.

21. Should the succession duty exoneration clause apply to all beneficiaries? Is the buy/sell agreement exclusion required?

22. Special instructions concerning burial, organ transplants, etc. Note that executors, next of kin, and physician should be made aware of these provisions.

23. Does testator wish to grant any powers of appointment?

24. Does testator wish to prepare any memoranda for the guidance of the trustees?

25. Consider inclusion of the following trustee powers:

    a) to retain infants' shares

    b) to make payments on behalf of infants

    c) to convert or retain original assets

    d) to divide in specie

    e) to invest in trustee or unrestricted investments

    f) to deal with real estate (maintenance, management, repair, disposal, options, etc.)

    g) to deal with share in corporations (same powers as testator when alive: voting, exercise of options, direction of management, etc.)

    h) to incorporate corporations

    i) to carry on a business or partnership

    j) to create separate trusts for business income for benefit of non-residents

    k) renew notes and guarantees, and to distinguish between capital and income receipts

    l) to borrow

    m) to buy estate assets, take remuneration, pass accounts, etc.

    n) to make all advantageous elections under the Income Tax Act and (if relevant) the Succession Duty Act.

ESTATE-PLANNING CONSIDERATIONS

1. Consider advisability of freezing part or whole of estate.

2. Estimate liabilities and consider method of payment.

3. Consider ownership and premium payor of life insurance.

4. Ascertain amount of income available to maintain the family after death.

5. Consider ownership of personal real estate.

6. Consider creation of charitable foundation.

7. Consider advisability of trusts for the children, either as estate-freezing devices, or to split income.

8. Consider advisability of agreements such as buy/sell agreements, voting trust agreements, etc.

9. If client should have any foreign source of income, consider whether any tax planning in Canada would be advantageous.

10. Consider purchase of an annuity for a charity.

11. Consider creation of holding corporation to defer income tax, change situs of assets, etc.

Documents Registry

List all documents and location of originals, and obtain copies of all relevant documentation.

TRUSTS

A trust is a legal agreement where one or more persons for the trustee holds title to property for the beneficiaries of the trust. The person who creates the trust is called the settlor. Thus, three people are involved.

A trust is not meant only for the will, or something to be done just for the elderly, nor is it excessively difficult to create. Trusts are valuable for family businesses, controlling family money and succession planning, and in avoiding taxation.

There are living trusts — inter vivos.

Trusts created by your will are called "testamentary trusts," and trusts for spouses are called "spousal trusts." These types are set up so that all of the income of the trust can be paid to the spouse during his or her lifetime, and only that spouse can access the capital. Assets are transferred to the trust at your cost and capital gains are only taxable when your spouse dies and the trust ends. The trust is always separate from your estate, if your estate creates a trust, and can continue for many years beyond your death.

A trust is a separate person that is taxed separately, yet you can control its operations and the future of your assets.

Family trusts are beneficial as you can establish one for 21 years when a trust is usually deemed to dispose of all of its property. This is currently under review by the Minister of Finance and has been extended for 20 years.

The usual type of family trust is the preferred beneficiary election plan where amounts of income from the trust are treated as if they are paid out to family members even though they are not actually paid. This is especially beneficial when family members have no other income or are at a low tax rate. Then, at the end of the trust, the money can be paid out free of tax.

Offshore Protection Trusts are beneficial for high-net-worth individuals exposed to significant liability. My preference is Cayman, Turks and Caicos, the Channel Islands or Bermuda. The trust holds the assets in a legal jurisdiction where a Canadian court judgement is not enforceable.

To set up a trust offshore, the minimum thresholds are usually $500,000 to $1,000,000 or more, and legal fees can easily run to $15,000 or more plus annual administration fees. The purpose cannot be fraudulent and you must be solvent at the time you do this.

Canadians are taxed on worldwide income so income earned may be taxable in Canada unless it is structured as a charitable trust or family trust.

Second property or recreational property trusts are used by families to pass on cottages or homes to children. If the property is given to the trust, there is no land transfer tax costs and it eliminates the capital gains tax on the property if it is a second home. There will be taxes, but the saving will be a lot greater. It is separate from the estate of the parents and exempt from probate fees.

Trusts for Income Splitting

This ideal way to transfer property to low-tax-rate family members to save taxes is an old one as we have described above. This truly benefits adult children, especially if there are reinvested dividends and capital gains, and dividend income from a family business that can flow through tax free to children who have no other income up to $24,000 a year.

With the ever-increasing onslaught to the family with higher taxes and possible estate taxes, the formation of trusts in Canada should increase at a dramatic rate for Conservative Investors.

THE ENDURING POWER OF ATTORNEY — WHY WE ALL NEED ONE

If you were to become incompetent at any time in your life because of an accident or ill health, what would happen? We would assume that family members would look after us according to our wishes and would be able to pay our bills and manage our assets. The will only impacts on death.

But this is certainly not the case. In many provinces, for example, if you are an adult and incapable of looking after your affairs for any reason, there is a Provincial

Trustee that steps in to take charge. Your family and spouse have no control or say unless you take steps to protect yourself in advance.

In addition, in January 1995, Ontario will enforce the already approved new bill, Substitute Decisions Act, that places all the control in the hands of the province even against the wishes of the family and established agreements. The disturbing problem here is that many people believe that all your spouse or children must do is to go to the bank with a letter from your lawyer declaring your incompetence and they will have power of attorney over your assets. The bank power of attorney is only in place for bank accounts and for no other matters. It applies only in the bank where it is written. It is meaningless in all other areas.

What is even more disturbing is that the mess is made worse and not better when the Provincial Trustee steps in to take charge. The Provincial Auditor General's report suggests that the Provincial Trustees may have mismanaged the situation in 55 per cent or more of the cases, causing loss of value to the estate. Imagine the provincial government running your affairs and not your family or spouse! It is a very frightening and disturbing situation.

Most police forces and associations in Ontario are asking their members to establish an "Enduring Power of Attorney" that will be registered and witnessed to come into effect for all of your affairs in the event of an unforeseen accident or illness. It covers all of your affairs, expresses your wishes and intent and has priority over government legislation, especially if it is put into effect before January 1, 1995. After this date, the same form will be able to be used to protect you long term.

Both you and your spouse will need one so that each of you will have a plan in place. The best option is the "Enduring Power of Attorney" kit from Fish & Associates, 7951 Yonge Street, Thornhill, Ontario, L3T 2C4, Telephone: Life Forms 1-800-676-0584. For a total charge of $40.00 (tax included), they will send you the kit, register on-line, provide a response line for questions and problems and respond to your bank or any other party who questions it when your spouse needs verification. This registration process is invaluable. You also receive a wallet card to carry with you as further evidence. A similar kit is available to B.C. residents.

The "Enduring Power of Attorney" is only in place while you are alive. Your will takes over at death.

I strongly recommend that every adult Ontario and B.C. resident do this. It is crucial to every personal financial plan.

A SUMMARY OF ESTATE-PLANNING OPTIONS

- Full rollover to spouse: It defers all capital gains so long as the surviving spouse is alive. In a cyclical downturn in the family firm's market value, it may be more prudent to waive that option and plan for heirs to face the tax bite immediately.
- Estate freezes: Reorganizing a family company so that future growth is transferred to the next generation on a tax-deferred basis, via a new class of shares.

Trusts are commonly set up to control the voting of the new shares and dispersal of income, and to protect the children against spousal litigation in the event of future marriage breakups.

- Partial freezes: The owner-operator can choose to participate in this new class of common shares, if you're not anxious to see your kids become wealthier than you during your lifetime.

- Life insurance: Especially if the founder is relatively young, this can be an answer as a capital gains hedge to enable the next generation to keep hold of the family business.

- Assets streaming: Diverting a family firm's liquid assets into a holding company. The holding company is a "creditor proofing" device that protects a percentage of the estate against future lawsuits aimed at the company.

- Split estates: This mechanism creates two taxpayers after death: the surviving spouse and the estate (via a continuing trust). The splitting of income between the two can save about $8,000 a year in tax on a $500,000 estate, and upward.

- RRSP carry-forwards: Even if you have a modest estate, you want a clause in the will empowering the trustee on behalf of your surviving spouse to make a registered retirement savings plan contribution in the year of your death, or even to carry forward unused RRSP contributions from previous years.

- Multiple wills: For Ontario residents, a separate will governing capital property (such as a family firm) may make sense, in order to exclude jointly owned assets from the "probate net." Why do that, you ask? Because the Ontario government in June 1992, increased its probate fees to $15 from $5 per thousand on estates worth $50,000 or more.

- Finally, prepare a proper will. Without one, the government takes command, and possible tax savings follow the individual to the grave.

TRUST CHECKLIST

A. *Inter vivos trusts:*

1) Value of property. Does it justify costs of creating trusts?

2) Risk of property from attack by creditors or others.

3) Future need for trust as in the case of educational prospects of children.

4) Complexity of trust — is it needed?

5) Validity of the trust — whether money has really been put under the administration of trustees.

B. *Testamentary trusts:*

1) If specific bequest in a will is reasonable and easy, then a trust may not be appropriate.

2) Is property sufficiently valuable to justify a trust?

3) Are there changing interests of heirs that the flexibility of a trust can better protect than a fixed bequest?

4) Is there a situation in which income should or can go to a spouse and remaining capital to children after the spouse's death?

5) Do you have suitable persons to act as trustees for assets?

OFFSHORE ASSET PROTECTION TRUSTS

The idea is to transfer assets to a trust outside your control. The trust must be irrevocable but able to be collapsed at some future date if it is no longer needed, with the proceeds going to the beneficiaries of the trust.

In Canada, an asset protection trust can be overturned by future creditors. Therefore, the offshore trust is placed in an environment where the trust cannot be overturned easily.

I recommend a threshold of $500,000 as a minimum to set up the trust. Set-up is $5,000 for your lawyers in Canada, $10,000 for the lawyers in the trust island you choose and 1 per cent a year of the value of the trust for administration.

Basic Rules

1) Banking secrecy laws in place with no currency controls.

2) Long-term protection against future creditors' ability to overturn the trust.

3) A tax-free environment — no tax treaty with Canada.

4) A safe haven, even a fun place to visit for holidays once a year. Cayman has great diving. Turks and Caicos Islands great beaches. They're all British.

5) Access via telephone, fax, airplane.

6) A friendly government or not much government at all.

CHAPTER TEN

The Power of Tax Planning

CONSERVATIVE STRATEGIES THAT REALLY WORK

The essence of proper tax planning is to preserve cash and maximize yields on income and investments. As asset preservation is a core element, tax planning is a critical and powerful tool for every Canadian investor.

All investment decisions have tax consequences and consume cash that could be otherwise used. To minimize the tax impact is important, but the investment decision must be made on the basis of the quality of the deal first, then liquidity and risk, then return, and finally the tax benefits or costs.

This process reduces the mistakes people make in being tax driven and preoccupied with tax minutiae instead of the quality of the deal.

There are many issues to consider in compiling a tax plan. These include:

- Income Splitting: Transferring income from a high to lower taxed person.

- Income Deferrals: Transfer income to a lower tax year.

- Defer Deductions: Transfer deductions from a low tax rate year to a high one.

- Tax Deferrals: Delaying the recognition and taxation of income.

- Tax Shelters: Tax low incentives to maximize deductions.

- Labour-Sponsored Venture Capital Corporations: Forty per cent to to 94 per cent credits.

- Special RRSP and RRIF transactions.

Table 10.1: Top Marginal Tax Rates 1994 (ranked highest to lowest)

TOP MARGINAL TAX RATES[1] (1994 – RANKED HIGHEST AND LOWEST)

	Dividends	Capital Gains	Other Income	Income Threshold[2]	1993 Ranking
British Columbia	36.6%	40.6%	54.2%	$79,400	5
Nova Scotia	36.3%	40.3%	53.8%	$81,140	8
Ontario	35.9%	39.9%	53.2%	$67,850	2
Quebec[3] (1993 budget)	38.7%	39.7%	52.9%	$63,395	1
Saskatchewan	36.5%	39.0%	52.0%	$63,395	3
New Brunswick	34.7%	38.5%	51.4%	$93,030	6
Newfoundland	34.7%	38.5%	51.3%	$63,395	4
Manitoba	36.3%	37.8%	50.4%	$63,395	7
Prince Edward Island	34.0%	37.7%	50.3%	$92,735	8
Yukon Territory	30.9%	34.9%	46.6%	$63,395	11
Alberta	31.4%	34.6%	46.1%	$63,395	10
Northwest Territories	30.0%	33.3%	44.4%	$63,395	12

Notes
1. The marginal tax rate is the rate of tax on the next dollar of income.
2. Top marginal tax rate applies when taxable income reaches these approximate threshold levels, assuming a base level of salary, the personal tax credit and the credits for CPP/QPP and Unemployment Insurance premiums.
3. Rate has remained unchanged.

Table 10.2: Personal Income Tax

	BASIC RATE	HIGH INCOME SURTAX	RETAIL SALES TAX	GAS TAX	SMALL BUSINESS TAX RATE
Alberta	45.5	8.0	–	9.0	6.0
British Columbia	62.6	30/50	7.0	11.0	10.0
Saskatchewan	50.0	18.0	9.0	15.0	8.5
Manitoba	52.0	2.0	7.0	11.5	10.0
Ontario	60.6	20/30	8.0	14.7	9.5
Quebec	n/a	n/a	8.0	14.5	5.75
New Brunswick	64.0	8.0	11.0	10.7	9.0
Nova Scotia	59.5	20/30	11.0	12.8	5.0
Prince Edward Island	59.5	10.0	10.0	10.7	7.5
Newfoundland	69.0	–	12.0	15.7	5.0

Table 10.3: A Comparison of Canadian and U.S. Taxes for Retired Couples

$U.S. INCOME	COUPLE A	COUPLE B
CPP and OAs	$20,000	$20,000
RRSP	$20,000	$40,000
Interest income	$10,000	$20,000
Total	$50,000	$80,000
Approximate tax if couple are Canadian citizens		
Canada	$11,000	$30,000
U.S.	–	–
Total tax	$11,000	$30,000
Approximate tax if couple are U.S. citizens		
Canadian withholding tax	$5,000	$6,000
U.S. income tax (after credit)	$1,000	$5,000
Total	$6,000	$11,000
Tax Saving if U.S. resident	$5,000	$19,000

Table 10.4: Personal Income Tax (ranking of the top combined federal and provincial marginal rate in per cent)

	1993	1994
British Columbia	51.1	54.2
Nova Scotia	50.3	53.8
Ontario	52.3	53.2
Quebec	52.9	52.9
Saskatchewan	51.9	51.9
New Brunswick	50.7	51.4
Newfoundland	51.3	51.3
Manitoba	50.4	50.4
Prince Edward Island	50.3	50.3
Yukon	46.5	46.5
Alberta	46.1	46.1
Northwest Territories	44.4	44.4

Source: Canadian Tax Foundation

The change in the age credit allowance is as follows:

Table 10.5: Change in the Age Credit Allowance

Income	1994		1995 AND SUBSEQUENT YEARS	
	Reduction in the age credit	Increase in federal and provincial tax	Reduction in the age credit	Increase in federal and provincial tax
$20,000	$0	$0	$0	$0
$25,000	$0	$0	$0	$0
$30,000	$306	$84	$612	$167
$35,000	$681	$187	$1,362	$373
$40,000	$1,056	$289	$2,112	$578
$45,000	$1,431	$392	$2,862	$783
$50,000	$1,741	$477	$3,482	$953
$75,000	$1,741	$492	$3,482	$983
$100,000	$1,741	$492	$3,482	$983

Table 10.6: Combined Federal-Provincial Marginal Tax Rates (%)

1994 Taxable Income	$6,750– 29,590	$29,591– 34,400[1]	$34,401– 40,560[2]	$40,561– 59,180[3]	$59,181 63,396[4]	$63,397 and over[5]
BRITISH COLUMBIA						
Salary	24.9	38.9	39.6	40.4/44.5	49.7	51.1/54.2
Interest	26.4	40.4	40.4	40.4/44.5	49.7	51.1/54.2
Dividends	7.1	24.6	24.6	24.6/27.1	33.5	51.1/54.2
Capital gains	19.8	30.3	30.3	30.3/33.4	37.3	38.3/40.6
ALBERTA						
Salary	24.3	37.7	38.3	39.1/40.1	44.6	46.1
Interest	25.8	39.1	39.1	39.1/40.1	44.6	46.1
Dividends	7.4	24.1	24.1	24.1/24.7	30.4	31.4
Capital gains	19.3	29.3	29.3	29.3/30.0	33.5	34.6
SASKATCHEWAN						
Salary	27.5	41.8	42.5/44.7	45.5	50.5	52.0
Interest	29.1	43.3	43.3/45.5	45.5	50.5	52.0
Dividends	10.0	27.8	27.8/29.3	29.3	35.5	36.5
Capital gains	21.8	32.5	32.5/34.2	34.2	37.9	39.0
MANITOBA						
Salary	26.9	40.8/42.8	43.5	44.3	49.0	50.4
Interest	28.4	42.3/44.3	44.3	44.3	49.0	50.4
Dividends	9.6	27.0/29.5	29.5	29.5	35.4	36.3
Capital gains	21.3	31.7/33.2	33.2	33.2	36.7	37.8

1994 Taxable Income	$6,750– 29,590	$29,591– 34,400[1]	$34,401– 40,560[2]	$40,561– 59,180[3]	$59,181 63,396[4]	$63,397 and over[5]
ONTARIO						
Salary	25.8	40.3	41.0	41.9/44.9	50.1	51.5/53.2
Interest	27.4	41.9	41.9	41.9/44.9	50.1	51.5/53.2
Dividends	7.4	25.5	25.5	25.5/27.3	33.8	34.8/35.9
Capital gains	20.5	31.4	31.4	31.4/33.7	37.5	38.6/39.9
NEW BRUNSWICK						
Salary	26.8	41.8	42.6	43.4	48.4	49.9/51.4
Interest	28.4	43.4	43.4	43.4	48.4	49.9/51.4
Dividends	7.7	26.4	26.4	26.4	32.7	33.7/34.7
Capital gains	21.3	32.6	32.6	32.6	36.3	37.4/38.5
NOVA SCOTIA						
Salary	26.1	40.7	41.4	42.3	47.1/50.6	52.0/53.8
Interest	27.6	42.3	42.3	42.3	47.1/50.6	52.0/53.8
Dividends	7.5	25.7	25.7	25.7	31.2/34.2	35.1/36.3
Capital gains	20.7	31.7	31.7	31.7	35.3/37.9	39.0/40.3
PRINCE EDWARD ISLAND						
Salary	26.1	40.7	41.4	42.3	47.1	48.6/50.3
Interest	27.6	42.3	42.3	42.3	47.1	48.6/50.3
Dividends	7.5	25.7	25.7	25.7	31.8	32.8/34.0
Capital gains	20.7	31.7	31.7	31.7	35.3	36.4/37.7
NEWFOUNDLAND						
Salary	27.6	43.1	43.8	44.7	49.9	51.3
Interest	29.2	44.7	44.7	44.7	49.9	51.3
Dividends	7.9	27.2	27.2	27.2	33.7	34.7
Capital gains	21.9	33.5	33.5	33.5	37.4	38.5
YUKON						
Salary	24.5	38.3	39.0	39.8	44.4/45.1	46.6
Interest	26.0	39.8	39.8	39.8	44.4/45.1	46.6
Dividends	7.0	24.2	24.2	24.2	30.0/30.5	31.4
Capital gains	19.5	29.8	29.8	29.8	33.3/33.8	34.9
NORTHWEST TERRITORIES						
Salary	23.7	37.1	37.7	38.5	42.9	44.4
Interest	25.2	38.5	38.5	38.5	42.9	44.4
Dividends	6.8	23.4	23.4	23.4	29.0	30.0
Capital gains	18.9	28.9	28.9	28.9	32.2	33.3

1. The threshold for Manitoba's secondary rates is $30,000.
2. The threshold for Saskatchewan's secondary rates is $40,363.
3. The thresholds for secondary rates in this bracket are: British Columbia – $54,632, Alberta – $45,390, Ontario – $52,276.
4. The thresholds for secondary rates in this bracket are: Nova Scotia – $60,859, Yukon – $61,674.
5. The thresholds for secondary rates in this bracket are: British Columbia – $79,404, Ontario – $67,854, New Brunswick – $93,029, Nova Scotia – $81,138, P.E.I. – $92,734.
Source: KPMG Peat Marwick Thorne

127

Clawbacks: The 1994 threshold for Old Age Security recipients is the same as 1993 — $53,215 of net income. Recipients repay benefits based on whichever is less: a) the amount received, or b) 15 per cent of net income over the threshold.

The net income thresholds for repayment of unemployment insurance benefits are $60,840 for 1994 and $58,110 for 1993.

Tax brackets and federal surtax: The three federal tax brackets are unchanged: $0-$29,590/$29,590-$59,180/$59,180-plus.

The federal individual surtax for 1994 will be 3 per cent of basic federal tax. The high-income surtax is unchanged at 5 per cent of basic federal tax over $12,500.

Provincial taxes:

British Columbia: Surtax rates increased to 30 per cent of B.C. tax in excess of $5,300 plus an additional 20 per cent on provincial tax over $9,000. Those rates were 20 per cent and 10 per cent in 1993.

Ontario: Surtax rates increased to 20 per cent of provincial tax in excess of $5,500 plus an additional 10 per cent on Ontario tax over $8,000. Those rates were 17 per cent and 8 per cent in 1993.

New Brunswick: The personal tax rate for 1994 will be 64 per cent of basic federal tax. That's up from 62 per cent in 1993.

Nova Scotia: Surtax rates will increase to 20 per cent of provincial tax in excess of $7,000 plus an additional 10 per cent on provincial tax over $10,499. Before, the surtax was just 10 per cent of Nova Scotia tax in excess of $10,000.

Maximum RRSP limit: $13,500 for 1994 and $12,500 for 1993.

Child-care expense deduction: No change, $5,000 per child under seven and $3,000 per child age seven to 14.

Basic personal amount: $6,456 for 1994 and 1993.

Age 65 credit: In 1994, this credit equalled $3,482. In 1995, this amount will be reduced for those seniors whose net income is greater than $25,921. For 1994, the age amount is reduced by 7.5 per cent of net income in excess of $25,921, and for 1995 and subsequent years, by 15 per cent of the net income in excess of this amount. This will result in an elimination of this age credit at an income level of $72,348 for 1994 and $49,134 for 1995 and subsequent years.

Disability amount: $4,233 for 1994 and 1993.

Medical expense threshold: $1,614 for 1994 and 1993.

Married amount: For 1994 and 1993, $5,380 if spouse's net income is up to $538. Partial credit may be available if spousal income is above that level.

Maximum Canada Pension Plan contribution: For 1994, $806 for employees and $1,612 for the self-employed. For 1993, $752.50 and $1,505.

Maximum Unemployment Insurance Premium: For 1994, $1,245.19. For 1993, $1,162.20.

INCOME SPLITTING — YES, YOU CAN!

Wouldn't it be great if you could split your income with a family member — whether a spouse or a child — who makes less money than you and have him or her invest it so that the income earned would be taxed at a lower rate? That's called income splitting, and it is a great idea.

Based on the budget measures and the accompanying White Paper proposals, which outline a reform plan for pensions and RRSPs in Canada, there is an even greater need to utilize an income splitting strategy for both spouses, establish separate RRSPs and investment income accounts and recognize that the new threshold for the Old Age Pension clawback will be $49,000 in 1995/1996.

However, a major consideration with respect to income splitting is what are known as attribution rules. These rules ensure that any income earned this way must be attributed back to the source — you — to be taxed at your rate. Still, income splitting can be done effectively in certain situations. Here's how.

- You can invest the child tax credit in a child's name without attribution.

- You can buy a child an equity-based mutual fund. There's no attribution on capital gains; that is, the profit realized when you sell an equity for more than you paid for it.

- Gifts from relatives outside of Canada are exempt from attribution.

- If you're lucky enough to be a two-income family that only needs the higher income to live on, then you can invest all of the lower income and have the interest earned taxed only at the lower-income earner's rate. This requires a separate bank account for each income earner — all expenses must be paid with the higher income, and all investments paid for with the lower income.

Table 10.7: Tax, Payment and Instalment Dates

IMPORTANT DATES TO REMEMBER

Last day for payments for	Dec. 31 1994	Jan. 30 1995	Mar. 1 1995	Apr. 30 1995
• charitable donations	√			
• medical expenses	√			
• union dues and professional fees	√			
• investment counsel fees, interest and other investment expenses	√			
• alimony and maintenance payments	√			
• child care expenses	√			
• moving expenses	√			
• political contributions	√			
• certain deductible legal fees	√			
• tuition fees for self	√			
• tax shelter investments	√			
• RRSP administration fees paid outside of self-administered plan	√			
• tax instalment for farmers and fishermen	√			
• any interest owing to you for 1994 on inter-family loans		√		
• any interest payable to you on loans from your employer, in order to reduce your taxable benefit		√		
• reimbursements to your employer to reduce your taxable operating benefit from an employer-provided automobile (due by February 14)		√		
• deductible contributions to your own RRSP or a spousal plan, including spousal rollover of pension income			√	
• contributions to federal or provincial labour-sponsored venture capital corporations and offer provincial plans			√	
Tax return filing deadline and date for payment of final balance of taxes and other amounts owing				√

Instalment Due Dates

In general, instalments for 1994, where applicable, are to be made no later than the 15th day of March, June, September and December, 1995.

130

Use tax shelters to withdraw money from your RRSP/RRIF in a tax-neutral transaction while building your cash flow and asset base.

A tax shelter that allows a $5,000 deduction in 1994 could be used to withdraw $20,000 from your RRSP with no further tax consequences. This can also be used to reduce your tax liability permanently.

LABOUR-SPONSORED VENTURE CAPITAL FUNDS (LSVCF)

These investment vehicles were designed by the government to allow smaller companies access to venture capital in order to grow their companies and create employment, and eventually a larger tax base. These funds take equity positions in smaller listed companies or in private companies that may be public at some future date. The investments are generally long-term oriented. Venture capital investments are generally riskier than most other investments, but venture capital funds pool much of the investors' money and invest it across many different investments and thus lower overall portfolio risk.

Several provinces such as Ontario, British Columbia, Saskatchewan and Prince Edward Island offer these programs.

The maximum annual investment is $5,000. Investors are given a $1,000 provincial tax credit and a further $1,000 federal tax credit when they complete their tax returns. In addition, these venture capital funds are 100 per cent RRSP eligible at their full face value of $5,000. If purchased as a $5,000 RRSP contribution, the investor would also receive the RRSP tax deduction of $5,000.

	50% TAX BRACKET (>$62,193)	42% TAX BRACKET (>$29,591)
Initial investment	$5,000	$5,000
Less: Federal Tax Credit	($1,000)	($1,000)
Provincial Tax Credit	($1,000)	($1,000)
Less: RRSP tax savings of		
$5,000 deduction	($2,500)	($2,100)
Real cost to investor	$500	$900
Real value as an investment	$5,000	$5,000

One hundred per cent financing is usually available to qualified investors, so your cash cost is the after-tax cost of money.

Venture capital pools are listed as mutual funds and are suitable for most RRSPs, but should be looked upon as long-term investments of at least five years or more. Government regulatory policy is to tax back a portion of the tax credit if the investment is sold within a five-year period. Retirees can withdraw their funds in two years if needed.

The most critical aspect of a venture capital pool investment is the quality of the investment management team.

Working Ventures, the biggest and oldest LSVCF, has over $288 million under administration. It has made 11 deals for a total of $32 million, and $10 million in deals are expected shortly. I consider this to be grossly inadequate and the returns have been quite poor considering the great advantage of lead time and federal grants this fund received. It needs to dramatically enhance its performance and conclude some excellent deals.

Another fund initiated in Ontario and sponsored by the Union of Commercial and Food Services Workers and the Labourers International Union has attracted close to $20 million in its first year and should double this in 1994-1995. Managed by Premier Capital of Toronto, a group of pure venture capitalists and merchant bankers, this fund targets technology, software, retail and innovative growth firms to supply equity and subordinated debt.

The more liberal rule passed in the Ontario budget will make it easier for these groups to place even more money in better businesses and get more invested more quickly.

Integrated Growth has placed a number of investments and should be substantially invested by the end of RRSP season.

A new fund has been started to invest in the electronic highway/CD ROM/television and cable industry, perhaps Canada's fastest growing sector. This fund — called the Active Communications Growth Fund — is sponsored by Actra, The Association of Canadian Television and Radio Artists. I suspect this fund will be very aggressively managed by Kingwest Investments of Toronto, an experienced portfolio manager that has selected a powerful collection for its board of directors drawn from television and film.

These funds are meant to be long-term holds — five years or more — but it is essential that you maximize the deductions and reduce your cash lost. If you can't use it for your RRSP and spousal RRSP, or are over 71, buy it to get the 40 per cent credit, as you can redeem in full in two years.

Since you are at risk, dollars are low but the yield is on the total investment; the actual cash on cash yield could be as high as 50 per cent if the fund does well. By law, 20 per cent must be kept in reserve in cash by the fund, yet your after-tax cash cost is only about 7 per cent. So the risk is definitely in your range.

MORE BUDGET CHANGES

The February 22nd federal budget announced significant changes that should impact on most Canadians. Most important is the $575-million tax increases we face. Most of this amount comes from the loss of the age exemption for those

Canadians over 65 years of age with more than $26,000 per year in taxable income, the retraction of the $100,000 lifetime capital gains exemption, the reduction in allowable claims for meals and entertainment expenses from 80 per cent to 50 per cent, and the new taxation of the first $25,000 in employer-provided life insurance coverage. The budget gives us the following personal financial warnings:

1) This is the first of a two-part budget; the second part will probably introduce the taxation of medical and dental benefits as is already the case in Ontario.

2) The $500,000 capital gains exemption for an incorporated business is under review and likely will be changed (not for the better).

3) The Canada Pension Plan and RRSP programs are under review and recommendations will be covered in a separate federal government White Paper. The most likely changes will be a gradual raising of age eligibility for the CPP, freezing (or even reducing) RRSP contribution limits, and reducing investment options eligible for RRSPs.

4) It is clear that with the reduction of the age exemption for Canadian seniors the new threshold for the clawback of Old Age Pension by the federal government will now be $49,000, down from $54,000.

5) It is obvious that as a result of these changes, both spouses will now need to own their own RRSP, separate investment portfolio and retirement and estate plans. Income splitting will be an essential element in this strategy to reduce taxes as the government obviously intends to tax the over-60s age group. The government recognizes that this group holds 60 per cent of all assets and disposable income in Canada. The middle age, middle class in Canada is broke and it can no longer afford to carry the burden of paying 60 per cent of all taxes that, up until now, have been collected in Canada.

6) The movement will be to increase taxes via "surtaxes" (i.e., taxes on taxes). Professor Michael Bliss, Professor of History at the University of Toronto, suggests in the February issue of *Canadian Business* that the top marginal tax rate in Canada will reach 75 per cent by 1999. This view is certainly supported by a recent OECD study which found that Canadians face the second-highest tax burden in the industrialized world (only the French are worse off). Tax planning has become essential for all family members.

7) The GST Review Committee, chaired by Toronto M.P. Jim Petersen, will recommend that the federal government eliminate the GST in its present form and consent to "burying" it in the price of all goods and services (similar in concept to the European V.A.T.), and "harmonizing" the range of goods and services it applies to (for example, frozen store-bought pizza and not just the delivery kind).

Table 10.8

PROJECTED REVENUE IMPACT OF SELECTED BUDGET CHANGES
(in millions of dollars)

	1994-95	1995-96	1996-97
Elimination of $10,000 lifetime capital gains exemption	$30	$415	$340
Life insurance benefits	$120	$200	$200
Age credit	$20	$170	$300
Home buyer's plan	-$15	-$55	-$60
Charitable donations credit	0	-$15	-$15
Total	$155	$715	$765

LIFETIME CAPITAL GAINS EXEMPTION (LCGE)

For real estate other than principal residence for the 1994 tax year, you will file a tax return on an investment or vacation or retirement property if you owned it prior to March 1992. The LCGE will be reduced by your Cumulative Net Investment Losses for all of 1994 which arise if you claimed interest expense on tax-shelter deductions or an allowable business investment loss after 1984.

If you eventually sell the second property at a loss, the loss will be reduced by any LCGE claimed under the election because of the alternative tax or clawback created by increasing your net income for tax purposes.

TAX SHELTERS

Most tax shelters are set up as a limited partnership you acquire on interest in an active business; you write off certain expenses plus the costs of selling up the partnership that are flowed through to the investor. Income then flows from the business back to the investor.

The important issues are the quality of the business in which you are investing and its management, liquidity, how you can get out of the deal in the future, and the tax benefits. They are really of benefit for those in the 50-plus per cent tax bracket.

Table 10.9: Tax Shelters

DEAL TYPE	TAX BENEFIT	HISTORY OF PERFORMANCE	LIQUIDITY
Film	30% per annum 90–100% financing	Poor	Cash recovery is rare
Mining and Oil and Gas Exploration Partnerships	Substantial write-offs especially in Quebec High risk	Good to Excellent	Positive annual cash flow and payout in 6–7 years
Mutual Fund Limited Partnership	50% in year one 100% financing	Excellent 10%+ after tax	Strong cash recovery and eventual buy back
Computer Software	Write-offs up to 100% in year one	Too soon to tell Could be mega hit	4-year term of public offering
Real Estate Limited Partnership	Depends on location. The U.S. ones are best	Multi-unit residential in the U.S. are best	Cash flow guarantees 100% rented

Things to watch out for:

1) Excess soft costs and high offering fees.

2) Is there real liquidity?

3) Track record of promoters.

4) When does the general partner get paid?

5) Are the cash flow guarantees covered by a letter of credit?

TAX TIPS FOR CONSERVATIVE INVESTORS

Integration of Investment

Income for 1994 and 1995*

Below is a summary of:

- the 1994 and 1995* tax savings/costs of flowing investment income (including capital gains) through a corporation; and

- the 1994 and 1995* tax deferral advantages/disadvantages when the after-tax investment income funds (including capital gains) are retained in a corporation, rather than paying them out as dividends to the shareholder(s).

These results are calculated as a percentage of the amount received and are based on the following assumptions.

- The individual is taxed at the top marginal tax bracket for 1994 and 1995.

- The dividends are received from taxable Canadian corporations.

- Investment income comprises interest, rents or royalties.

135

Table 10.10: Summary of Tax Savings/Costs of Flowing Investment Income and Tax Deferral Advantages/Disadvantages

Province	Dividends Tax Deferral 1995[1]	1994	Investment Savings/ (Costs)	Income Tax Deferral	Capital Gains Savings/ (Costs)	Capital Gains Tax Deferral
British Columbia	3.24%	11.57%	0.40%	8.90%	0.30%	6.60%
Alberta	(1.93)	6.40	(2.90)	1.80	(2.30)	1.30
Saskatchewan	3.18	11.51	(2.20)	6.10	(1.70)	4.60
Manitoba	3.00	11.33	(3.60)	4.60	(2.80)	3.40
Ontario	2.59	10.92	0.80	8.90	0.50	6.60
Quebec	5.39	13.72	(2.20)	7.80	(1.70)	5.90
New Brunswick	1.35	9.68	(1.40)	5.60	(1.20)	4.10
P.E.I.	0.64	8.97	(0.20)	6.50	(0.30)	4.80
Nova Scotia	2.97	11.30	0.60	8.90	0.50	6.70
Newfoundland	1.33	9.66	(0.60)	6.50	(0.40)	4.90

The deferral is equal to the difference of the after-tax cash retained by a corporation compared to an individual who earns the investment income (including capital gains). For example, in the case of $1,000 of interest earned in the province of Ontario.

	Individual Earns the Income	Corporation Earns the Income	Difference
Interest	$1,000	$1,000	
Taxes at top marginal personal rate	(532)	N/A	
Part I tax — corporate	N/A	(443)	
After-tax cash	$468	$557	$89

The difference/deferral of $89 expressed as a percentage translates into 8.9 per cent as shown in the table above.

*Assuming that there are no tax increases.

(1) Assuming that the 1994 budget proposal to increase the Part IV tax to 33 1/3 per cent is enacted substantially in its existing form.

MECHANICS: CAPITAL GAINS EXEMPTION ELECTION

Facts:

- Cottage purchased on January 1, 1982 for $100,000 (ACB).

- City place is the principal residence.

- Fair market value of the cottage on February 22, 1994 is $300,000.

- The entire $100,000 capital gains exemption is available.

- The cumulative net investment loss (CNIL) is nil.

Results:

- Holding Period Information:

—Number of months property owned up to February 1994	146
—Number of months property owned after February 1992	24

- Tax Return:

—Deemed proceeds	$219,672
—Less: ACB	100,000
—Deemed gain	119,672
—Taxable portion	89,754
—Deduction re: post-February 1992 gain	14,75*
—Deduction in arriving at taxable income	$ 75,000

- New ACB of property ($100,000 + $100,000) $200,000

$$* \frac{24}{146} \times 119,672 \times 75\%$$

BASIC TAX TIPS

1) Loan money to a spouse or family member at the prescribed rate for investments if they are at a lower tax rate. The prescribed rate of interest stays in effect for the term of the loan. For example, in the second quarter of 1994 the rate was 4 per cent. For the third quarter it was to be 6 per cent. The 4 per cent is in effect for the entire term of the loan. As long as interest is paid on the loan 30 days after year-end, there is no attribution back to you.

2) Business income from a small business or home business is not attributed. Sales to a spouse at fair market value are not subject to the rules if you receive adequate payment in return. Transfers of property between spouses are generally considered to be made at your adjusted cost base of the property. You can elect on your tax return to make the transfer at fair market value rather than at the cost base.

3) If you are at a higher tax rate than your spouse and pay off his or her credit cards, there is no attribution while it is a gift and if it is to pay off normal costs.

4) Changes to regulations on RRIFs came into effect after 1992. The rules were amended to allow payments to be made until the death of the individual or their spouse rather than ending at age 90. There is a minimum amount required to be withdrawn each year, but you can withdraw as much as you want when you want.

The minimum for year 1 is 7.38 per cent and year 2 is 7.48 per cent. After age 94, you must take out 20 per cent of the value of the fund at the beginning of each year.

If you purchased a RRIF before 1993, the lower rates apply for those aged up to 77. The new high rates apply for all RRIFs for ages above 71 regardless of when purchased.

If you have a younger spouse, set up a new RRIF. Minimum payments on the new one can be based on the younger spouse's age. The payments will be smaller, but will stretch out for many more years.

5) Until the end of 1994, you may transfer up to $6,000 to a spousal RRSP from payments you receive from a registered pension plan or deferred profit-sharing plan. This will allow the spouse to claim the pension income tax credit and receive the pension income personally, probably at a lower tax rate.

6) To receive the Child Care Tax Benefit, you and your spouse must both file a tax return every year.

7) For the GST Tax Credit or Child Tax Benefit, request that the amounts be electronically deposited directly into a bank account set up for investment purposes. This can be done for the child and investment income earned on it will be taxed only in their hands.

8) For single parents with a child under 18 earning income from part-time employment, establish an RRSP for the child and let the investment income accrue tax free. The child must file a return.

9) If you have a substantial investment income and you are in a top marginal tax rate, you may be better off accruing the investment income inside a holding corporation. These are usually taxed at a lower corporation rate of, say, 44 per cent instead of your rate at, say, 53 per cent.

This method is beneficial if you plan to leave in the holding corporation for a period of time and not pay it out in dividends. Changes in the budget of 1994 altered the deferral benefit and tax savings for some provincial jurisdictions.

10) Be aware of anti-avoidance rules.

a) Loan Guarantees: If you arrange a bank loan for a third party to borrow money for investments, it will be treated as a direct loan by you.

b) Back-to-Back Loans: If you lend money to a spouse who in turn lends it to a child, it is treated as a direct loan by you.

c) Paying off a Loan: If you lend money to a spouse to pay off a loan, the loan will be treated as if it was yours and the income earned from the investments purchased by the original loan will be attributed to you.

d) There is a General Anti-Avoidance Rule (GAAR). If all the tricks you try are not caught by specific provisions of anti-avoidance, you will be caught by the general rule which applies to almost anything else you can think of.

e) Substituted Property Rate: If property is substituted for other loaned or transferred property, the income earned will be subject to attribution from the substituted property. If you give stock to your spouse who buys bonds and the spouse sells the stock to purchase the bonds, the interest income from the bonds will be attributed back to you.

DO WE TAX AND ESTATE PLAN TO AVOID PROBATE FEES, OR WHAT?

As a final tax comment, it should be noted that earlier in the estate chapter I mentioned specific ways to cut probate fees on the estate. This is especially relevant to residents of Ontario with its high rates.

However, it is usually wrong to make short-term decisions to avoid taxes and create long-term liability for the survivors. In other words, two well-known Canadian tax lawyers have said that it is wrong to "Probate Fee Plan" instead of properly estate plan.

Howard Carr and Suzanne Hanson, tax and estate law specialists, have both produced papers on the subject. What happens if you probate plan and transfer assets to spouses before death only to find that Ontario brings in a capital or wealth tax? You probably have doubled the tax for your survivor if this happens. What we are doing in avoiding probate fees and saving $10,000 to $15,000 is more often than not creating capital gain or additional tax liability for the family after your death that may be dramatically greater in the long term.

Probate planning to avoid fees on death is a short-term issue versus total tax on the estate, its capital, and the income to family members (the beneficiaries) which is long term. We as Conservative Investors should always think long term. Yet every tax book I have read and many of the seminars I have seen advertised, including ones involving national accounting firms, promote "ways to avoid probate fees." This is not proper financial planning.

CHAPTER ELEVEN

A Final Word or Two

This book has been designed and researched to be like no other. It was designed to protect and conserve the wealth of this country and to present new ideas that reduce risk and enhance returns.

This book has also been about the true power of money — how you can protect yourself and your family, conserve what you have and use that power for the good you have intended.

Power comes from knowledge and understanding. It must be dynamic and be used for good purposes. Canadians deserve to have the power.

The United Nations study of the quality of life factors and GDP rated Canada number one in the world out of 173 countries in 1994. Not bad!

The question remains as to how we can keep it this way.

There is nothing wrong with being financially successful in Canada. It is not something we must apologize for. Being diligent, conservative and responsible are the qualities a society should value most highly and encourage among its citizenry.

The government has now targeted the older, more conservative and financially responsible for new waves of taxation and estate taxes. Control over retirement and your property is being seriously threatened.

We have a great society threatened by disillusion and political break-up. We believe *The Power of Money* is also about hope, the future and the long-term well-being of its people.

I love Canada, and Canadians, because they are the "best people on earth" who deserve better. This book has been about more and better, a superior sense of personal security, sense of direction, a clear vision of the future, control over your destiny. This is the ultimate power in life.

The Power of Money is meant to support you in your relationship with your broker, financial planner, insurance agent, tax accountant and lawyer. It is not meant to replace their role, but only to make you more knowledgeable, and more effective, as an investor.

The Power of Money is also about fun. All of the above issues are meant to be realized while you enjoy them. Have a great life!

Glossary of Some Key Investment Terms

annual meeting A stockholder meeting, normally held at the same time each year, to elect the company's board of directors and transact other business.

arbitrage The practice of buying and selling two separate but related securities to profit from the difference in their values. An arbitrage opportunity often arises when two companies plan to merge or when one security is converted into another.

asset Anything of value owned by a company. Assets can include cash, product inventory and other current assets, as well as land, buildings, equipment.

averaging down The purchase of additional shares of already owned stock at lower prices to reduce the average cost per share of all shares held.

balance sheet A financial statement showing the company's assets (what the company owns), its liabilities (what it owes), and the difference, called "net worth" or "stockholders' equity."

bear market An extended declining trend in stock prices occurring usually in a time period of months or years.

beta Second letter of the Greek alphabet used by Wall Street to describe the volatility of a stock relative to a stock market index. Beta is regarded by some as a measure of a stock's market risk.

block A large amount of stock sold as a single unit. The term is most often used to describe a unit of 1,000 shares or more.

book value The equity value of an outstanding share of stock. Book value is determined by dividing the amount of stockholders' equity to which each share is entitled by the number of shares outstanding.

call option A contract giving the holder a right to buy 100 shares of a stock at a predetermined price (called the striking price) any time up to a predetermined expiration date. A call option is bought to profit by a rise in the stock's price.

capital gain A gain realized on the sale or exchange of securities, fixed property, or similar assets. Under current rules, the gain is taxable at a rate of up to 38 per cent.

capital loss A loss realized on the sale or exchange of securities, fixed property, or similar assets. The loss can sometimes be used to reduce taxes.

closed-end fund An investment company with a limited number of shares. To buy or sell, a shareholder must buy from or sell to another person, rather than deal directly with the investment company.

convertible debenture A debenture that is convertible into common shares at the option of the owner.

convertible preferred stock A preferred stock that is convertible into common shares at the option of the owner.

deflation The economic condition of falling prices for goods and services. Deflation, the inverse to inflation, refers to the increasing buying power of cash and a substantially reduced amount of currency in circulation.

depreciation The estimated decrease in value of property due to use, deterioration, or obsolescence over a period of time. Although depreciation does not require a cash outlay, it is a cost of doing business.

dividend A payment to stockholders, usually in the form of a quarterly cheque. The dividend is declared by the board of directors and is normally determined by the level of the company's earnings.

discount The amount below the list price or face value. A bond discount refers to the excess of the face value over its current market price. A bond that sells below 100 (below par) is said to be "selling at a discount."

dollar-cost-averaging An investment approach that involves consistently buying uniform dollar amounts of a security regardless of the price. When prices are low, more shares are bought than when prices are high.

fundamentalist One who believes that stock prices are determined by the future course of earnings and dividends. The fundamentalist studies, among other things, economics, industry conditions and corporate financial statements.

going public A term used to describe the initial sale of shares of a privately held company to the public for the first time. In recent years, the term "Initial Public Offering" (IPO) has, instead, become more popular.

inflation The economic condition of rising prices for goods and services. Inflation refers to a declining buying power of cash and a substantially greater amount of currency in circulation. It is generally the result of excessive government spending.

institutional investor A bank, mutual fund, pension fund, insurance company, university or other institution that invests in the securities markets.

interest The compensation a borrower pays a lender for the use of money borrowed.

junk bonds Bonds that are issued having little or no collateral or liquidation value. Junk bonds typically offer high interest income and very high risk. Bonds of this type have been popular instruments in buyouts, corporate mergers and acquisitions.

leveraged buyout Acquiring control of a company, usually using debt. Typically, the stock is purchased by employees or a group of investors with the help of an investment banker.

load mutual fund An open-end investment company that charges the investor a fee when the investor buys the fund shares. This fee (or "load," as it is called) is used primarily to compensate salespeople selling the fund.

margin account An account, typically with a brokerage firm, that allows an investor to buy or sell securities on credit. An investor can sometimes borrow up to 50 per cent or more of the investment value.

mutual fund An open-end investment company. A mutual fund offers the investor the benefits of portfolio diversification (i.e., owning more shares to provide greater safety and reduce volatility).

NASDAQ (pronounced "nazdak") The computerized National Association of Securities Dealers Automatic Quotation system that provides brokers and dealers with price quotations of securities traded over-the-counter.

no-load mutual fund An open-end investment company that allows investors to buy and sell fund shares without paying a fee (called the "load"). A no-load fund is sold by word-of-mouth and advertising since it typically has no salespeople.

open-end investment company An investment company that uses its capital to invest in other companies. Its shareholders can participate directly because the open-end investment company will sell or rebuy its own shares at book value. See also "mutual fund."

over-the-counter The nationwide network of brokers/dealers engaged in buying and selling securities that, for the most part, are not listed on exchanges.

paper profit A profit that has not been realized. In most cases, the term "paper profit" refers to the profit an investor has on a security that was purchased earlier but has not yet been sold.

preferred stock A stock that has prior claim on dividends (and/or assets in the case of corporate dissolution) up to a certain amount before the common stockholders are entitled to anything.

premium The amount above the list price or face value. A bond premium refers to the excess of the market price over its face value. A bond that sells above 100 (above par) is said to be "selling at a premium."

program trading Using a computer-driven program to buy and sell stocks. The objective is to capture the arbitrage profits available when, for example, stock indexes and their futures are being traded.

prospectus A document issued by a corporation at the time securities are offered providing buyers or potential buyers with pertinent details and data on the corporation and the security being issued. Also see "red herring."

proxy A written authorization by a stockholder allowing a representative or someone else to vote for or against directors and business proposals at the annual meeting. The results of these votes are usually announced at the meeting.

random walk A stock market theory based on the belief that stock price movements are completely random and unpredictable.

red herring A preliminary prospectus easily identified because much of the cover is printed in red as a warning to investors that the document is not complete or final.

retained earnings Earnings that have been reinvested back into the business after dividends are paid to stockholders. Retained earnings is often an important component of a company's stockholders' equity. Another name for retained earnings is "earned surplus."

retention rate The per cent of net earnings available for reinvestment into the company after dividends are paid to stockholders. The retention rate is also the inverse of the payout ratio. If the payout ratio is 25 per cent, the retention rate is 75 per cent.

return on equity The rate of investment return a company earns on stockholders' equity. Return on equity is calculated by dividing net earnings by average stockholders' equity.

short sale A trading technique typically used when a stock is expected to decline in price. A short sale involves selling borrowed stock anticipating that the same number of shares will be repurchased later at a lower price. The repurchased shares are then returned to the owner from whom they were borrowed.

technician or technical analyst One who studies all factors related to the actual supply and demand of stocks, bonds, or commodities. The primary tools of a technician are stock charts and various technical indicators.

triple witch The day on which stock options, stock index options, and stock index futures all expire simultaneously.

warrant A certificate giving the holder the right to purchase securities at a predetermined price within a predetermined time limit or perpetually. Warrants are issued directly by the company. In contrast, call options are written on stock already outstanding.

yield The annual return on an investment (from dividends or interest) expressed as a percentage of either cost or current price.

The Software Package

W hy include computer software with a book? The answer is simple: we want you to succeed! This means you must act and not react; plan and not think about planning; and take charge by building your personal financial data base.

The software is 100 per cent Canadian. By Canadians, for Canadians. It is custom-designed to service the needs of the Conservative Investor by supplying you with a comprehensive collection of tools, information, tables and forms to get the job done.

It is user-friendly and exceptionally simple to use. If you have a problem, you can call us or get one of your children or grandchildren to show you how. And please remember making money and preserving your wealth can be fun. That's F-U-N.

THE PROGRAM

We have assembled an exciting collection of Conservative Investor tools to protect you, inform and aid in decision-making. We start with a simple glossary of terms to ensure we all speak the same language. This is followed by a collection of goals and financial objectives to start to get you focused. We then begin to assemble a portrait of who we are, what we have and our risk orientation. We build custom models of asset allocation and calculate our interest expenses and costs.

We have included all federal and provincial tax tables to help you calculate your tax costs using various scenarios of interest, dividends and capital gains.

To complete our profiles, we assist you in calculating mortgage costs and insurance costs, and present the alternatives of using reverse mortgages over systematic withdrawal plans which we favour.

As you accumulate wealth, there are lists of foreign tax havens, as well as materials and texts on wills, estate planning, implications of dying intestate and special considerations for high-net-worth individuals.

Interactive Features of a Company Software Disk

1) Glossary of Investment Terms and Financial Planning Tools
2) Personal Goal Setting and Financial Objectives
3) Personal Net Worth Statement
4) Investor Risk Tolerance Profile
5) Suggested Asset Allocation Model
6) Personal Debt Service Threshold Calculation
7) Comparative Investment Fee Schedules
8) Canadian Federal and Provincial Tax Tables and Tax Treatment of Income Streams (Interest vs. Dividends vs. Capital Gains)
9) Comparison of Tax Sheltered vs. Non-Tax Sheltered Income
10) Mortgages, Amortization Tables and Mortgage Prepayment Calculations
11) Reverse Mortgage Calculations
12) Insurance Plan Options
13) Future Value Calculations of Present Dollars
14) Registered Retirement Income Fund (RRIF) Tables
15) Systematic Withdrawal Plans
16) Special Considerations for High-Net-Worth Individuals
17) List of Foreign Tax Havens
18) Implications of Dying Intestate
19) Estate-Planning Guidelines
20) Wills

The software menu is an exciting collection of options and calculations.

You may want to consider adding to your software collection by utilizing *Wealth Creator and Portfolio Tracker* also produced by RAM Technologies of Canada. Both are widely used by the leading financial planners and top brokers in the field. The consumer version is low cost but essential to your financial future. Take charge, choose wealth and get the power.

FOR TECHNICAL SUPPORT, PLEASE CONTACT:
RAM Technologies Inc.
964 Westport Crescent
Unit 14
Mississauga, Ontario
L5T 1S3
(905) 795 - 9222